# ENRICHING PRIMARY MATHEMATICS with IT

**Janet Ainley**

**Series Editor: Shirley Clarke**

Hodder & Stoughton

A MEMBER OF THE HODDER HEADLINE GROUP

*For Lilian, and her grandparents*

*British Library Cataloguing in Publication Data*

Ainley, Janet
  Enriching primary mathemtics with IT. – (Managing primary mathematics)
  1.Mathematics – Study and teaching (Elementary) – Data processing
  2.Mathematics – Data processing
  I.Title
  372.7'0285

ISBN 0 340 64402 8

First published 1996
Impression number     10  9  8  7  6  5  4  3  2  1
Year                  1999   1998   1997   1996

Typeset by Multiplex Techniques, Orpington, Kent.
Printed in Great Britain for Hodder & Stoughton Educational, a division of Hodder Headline Plc, 338 Euston Road, London NW1 3BH, The Bath Press

# CONTENTS

# ACKNOWLEDGMENTS

This book would not have been possible without the help of my colleague Dave Pratt, and the wonderful teachers and children involved in the Primary Laptop Project. Much of their work appears in the text, although names and particular circumstances have been changed.

I am very grateful to Ronnie Goldstein and Jane Arthurs for their comments on earlier drafts, and for their encouragement and enthusiasm.

Special thanks to Barry Poultney for taking the photographs.

# SOURCES OF HELP

The following organisations are amongst those who produce materials and publications in the area of using IT in mathematics.

**The Association for Teachers of Mathematics** (ATM) publishes two journals, *Mathematics Teaching* and *Micromath. Micromath* is concerned specifically with the use of IT in the learning and teaching of mathematics, and often has special features on particular applications.

ATM also produces a range of publications on various aspects of learning mathematics, including some software.

ATM, 7 Shaftesbury Street, Derby, DE23 8YB. Tel: 01332 346599

**The Mathematical Association** (MA) also produces a range of publications for teachers. Their journal *Mathematics in Schools* often features articles relating to the use of IT.

MA, 259 London Road, Leicester, LE2 3BE. Tel: 01162 703877

**The National Council for Educational Technology** (NCET) produces materials relating to the use of IT in many areas of the curriculum, as well as running projects of various kinds.

In particular, they produce information about software for primary mathematics, which is often circulated via LEAs to schools in the UK.

NCET, Milburn Hill Road, Science Park, Coventry, CV4 7JJ. Tel: 01203 416994

# INTRODUCTION

Even though computers are no longer a novelty in primary schools, their use is still relatively limited. The use of word processing has developed considerably, but many schools are only just beginning to explore the ways in which other kinds of software may be used across the whole primary curriculum. This book aims to help teachers to redress this balance, and to begin to exploit the real power that computers offer to support and enrich children's experience of mathematics.

Technology is developing very rapidly: new hardware and software are appearing at such a rate that it is easy to feel overwhelmed by the amount of new information that is available. There is no need to panic. You don't need to be up to date with the very latest ideas to read on. This book focuses on computer applications which are familiar and easily available. The new ideas which it offers are about ways of using the computer, and insights about children's learning, rather than about the latest technological developments.

## COMPUTERS AND MATHEMATICS

Increasingly, computers are being used as tools for doing mathematics. Both research mathematicians, and those who apply their knowledge in commercial and scientific contexts, rely on computer technology to make their work more accurate and efficient.

Computers can be equally powerful tools for those who are learning mathematics. They offer new ways of working and different kinds of support for learning. They can complement your skills as a teacher, but they can't replace them.

### More power

Computers have the ability to carry out calculations and routines quickly and accurately, so they make it possible to look at many results in a short space of time, or to see several examples at once. When you don't need to wade through routine calculations, you have more time to spend looking beyond the particular examples to think about general patterns and results. For example, if you can draw several different graphs in a few minutes, you can get a sense of the overall picture, and what information the graphs contain.

## Different ways of seeing

With a computer you can often see familiar things in new ways. You can have a table of data, and graphs drawn from it side by side. You can produce shapes and patterns from a list of numbers and instructions. You can sort and organise information in a whole variety of ways.

This can help learners to make links between different areas of mathematics, and between mathematics and other curriculum areas.

What is more, many of the images the computer offers are dynamic: you can control and alter them in ways that would be impossible in other media. You can create a rectangle, and then pull it to change its dimensions, or stretch a graph and watch the scales change on the axes. These are powerful experiences for forming new concepts.

## Formalising ideas

Despite the futuristic images we sometimes see of computers that converse like humans, any current software still responds only to a very restricted range of instructions, which you either have to type in, or select from menus. Computers still do what you tell them to do, rather than what you want them to do! There are times when this can seem like a real problem; you can't make the computer understand, and it is easy to lose your temper, or pull out the plug. In some software, the ways in which you give instructions can seem random and hard to remember.

However, in software which uses mathematical notation and vocabulary, this apparent restriction can prove to be a valuable learning aid. Written mathematics uses formal conventions of notation, which many children find difficult to master. Communicating with a computer provides a purpose for learning to use formal notation, and feedback about whether you have used it correctly, in a way which is not normally possible in other school contexts. The computer can form a valuable bridge between children's intuitive ideas and the formal world of mathematics.

# What help do *you* need?

This book has been organised in two sections which have quite different aims. You may feel that you don't know much about working with mathematical software, and that you need some help to develop your own skills and confidence. Section A *Getting to know about IT in mathematics* has been written to give an overview of what you can do with calculators, spreadsheets, databases, Logo and graphics packages. You will probably want to dip into this section of the book, picking out items which interest you, or which are unfamiliar, and skipping over bits you already know about.

It would be impossible in a single book to give detailed instructions for using specific pieces of software. Instead there is a general description, giving suggestions for activities which will help you to get started. To get the most out of this section of the book, you should try to plan some time to work on the computer in peace on your own, or better still with a friend or colleague. You will need to use the handbook for the particular software you have available to supplement the help given in each of the chapters, though of course it would be better still to find someone who knows the software and can offer you some support.

FIGURE 1   *Working with a colleague is the best support*

At the end of each chapter you will find references to classroom activities using that application which are described in Section B. A short list of further reading, for those who want to find out more about the area, can be found at the end of the book. See contents page for details.

Section B, *Using IT in classroom activities,* is written in quite a different way to complement the focus on separate applications in Section A. It begins with a chapter which looks at some issues to do with managing IT within the school and the classroom. It includes some examples of strategies which teachers have found effective in promoting the use of IT in mathematics, but also deals with some more general areas.

Each of the remaining chapters in Section B is based on a theme around which work might be planned in a primary classroom. Starting with familiar activities, ideas are offered to show how the power of IT might enrich children's mathematical experience.

Ideas are sequenced to show a mathematical progression, and are often illustrated by case studies describing children's work and teachers' responses. From working with activities like these in school, it is clear that the calculator or computer can allow children to tackle more sophisticated mathematical ideas than we might expect for their age. This makes it difficult to pin activities down to a particular age group. The activities are divided into two broad sections, aimed at 4- to 7-year-olds (Key Stage 1) and 7- to 11-year-olds (Key Stage 2), but *not* linked to specific age groups. In fact even the division between Key Stages is rather fuzzy, and there will be activities which may be appropriate for older or younger children as well.

After each activity is a box highlighting the key mathematical ideas in the activity. These will be relevant to all teachers, but they are also followed by specific references to Programmes of Study in the mathematics National Curriculum for England and Wales.

# SECTION A

## GETTING TO KNOW ABOUT IT IN MATHEMATICS

This section is divided into five chapters:

**CHAPTER 1**
Working with a calculator

**CHAPTER 2**
Working with a database

**CHAPTER 3**
Working with a spreadsheet

**CHAPTER 4**
Working with Logo

**CHAPTER 5**
Working mathematically with a graphics package

# WORKING WITH A CALCULATOR

> The purpose of this chapter is
> - to show you some new things you can do with an ordinary calculator;
> - to introduce some differences between types of calculators.

You will get most out of this chapter if you use a calculator to try out some of the activities and challenges as you read. It doesn't matter which kind of calculator you use: if you have more than one, try the activities on different calculators and see what happens.

## CALCULATORS IN THE CLASSROOM

Although calculators have become commonplace in the world outside school, there is still no universal agreement about their use in primary classrooms. It would not be appropriate to repeat here the various arguments that are made both for and against the use of calculators in primary schools, but it would be naive simply to ignore the anxieties which some parents and teachers have about their use. Such anxieties may perhaps arise from the idea that introducing calculators into the classroom means just that: having calculators around, but keeping everything else the same.

The image of children working through a traditional page of 'sums', but using a calculator is indeed a worrying one, but it is not the one which those who support the use of calculators would recognise. Like any new tool, the calculator allows us to do the old jobs, like long multiplication, more quickly and easily, but more importantly it makes it possible to tackle new and different jobs. We might think of a calculator both as a tool for getting answers *and* as a resource for learning mathematics. By giving thought to the new activities that we offer to children, it is possible to open up and enrich their experiences of doing mathematics.

In the following section, there are a number of activities which illustrate four different kinds of activities which exploit the power of calculators. Before you read on, go and find your calculator so that you can try some of them out.

# FOUR STARTING POINTS FOR THINKING ABOUT CALCULATORS

## *Trying lots of examples*

Calculators allow us to produce results quickly and accurately, so they make it easy to try out lots of examples and investigate patterns.

---

### Hundred squares

You will need a 'hundred square', like this.

| 0 | 1 | 2 | 3 | 4 | 5 | 6 | 7 | 8 | 9 |
|---|---|---|---|---|---|---|---|---|---|
| 10 | 11 | 12 | 13 | 14 | 15 | 16 | 17 | 18 | 19 |
| 20 | 21 | 22 | 23 | 24 | 25 | 26 | 27 | 28 | 29 |
| 30 | 31 | 32 | 33 | 34 | 35 | 36 | 37 | 38 | 39 |
| 40 | 41 | 42 | 43 | 44 | 45 | 46 | 47 | 48 | 49 |
| 50 | 51 | 52 | 53 | 54 | 55 | 56 | 57 | 58 | 59 |
| 60 | 61 | 62 | 63 | 64 | 65 | 66 | 67 | 68 | 69 |
| 70 | 71 | 72 | 73 | 74 | 75 | 76 | 77 | 78 | 79 |
| 80 | 81 | 82 | 83 | 84 | 85 | 86 | 87 | 88 | 89 |
| 90 | 91 | 92 | 93 | 94 | 95 | 96 | 97 | 98 | 99 |

- Choose a 2 by 2 square anywhere on your hundred square.
- Add the number in the top left corner to the one in the bottom right corner. Then add the numbers on the other diagonal.
- Try the same thing with other 2 by 2 squares. Can you explain what is happening?

As you try more examples, you may start to be able to predict the results you will get. If you are feeling confident, try extending the activity.

- Try doing the same activity with a 3 by 3 square ... or a 4 by 4 square ...
- Go back to a 2 by 2 square, but this time multiply the diagonals.
- What happens if you use a multiplication square instead of a hundred square?

**What other questions could you ask to extend this activity?**

Trying lots of examples can be an important stage in coming to understand a mathematical problem. As you worked on this activity you might have noticed your thoughts about the patterns changing as you became more confident of the results. Getting a sense of what is happening is the first step towards being able to explain the underlying mathematics, but of course the calculator does not help you to explain. The calculator is supporting mathematical thinking, but not replacing it.

The next activity is perhaps a little harder, and involves the idea of square numbers. However, with the calculator, it is just as easy to get started. How do your feelings about the problem change as you try more examples?

---

## Give and take
- - - - - - - - - - - - - - - -
$5^2 - 5 = 4^2 + 4$

$7^2 - 7 = 6^2 + 6$

$9^2 - 9 = 8^2 + 8$

- Does this pattern continue?
- If so, can you say why?
- If not, say when it does hold.

---

You may have approached this activity by simply continuing the sequence of counting numbers, using 10, 11, 12 and so on. How many examples did it take until you were convinced? But what about trying some really awkward numbers?

**Choose the most awkward numbers you can think of: can you make the pattern break down?**

Again, trying lots of examples may give you a sense of *what* is happening, but it will not tell you why it is happening. In order to do that you may need to look at a general case, rather than lots of specific ones. If you want to try finding an explanation for yourself, don't read on just yet.

If you would like some help with an explanation, this box may be useful.

To think about what is happening for *any* number, let's call the two numbers in the problem n and (n + 1).

The pattern tells us that

$$(n + 1)^2 - (n + 1) = n^2 + n$$

We need to look at each side of the equation separately:

| | |
|---|---|
| $(n + 1)^2 - (n + 1)$ | *we start with the left-hand side* |
| $= (n + 1) \times (n + 1) - (n + 1)$ | *this is just writing out squaring (n +1 ) in full* |
| $= n^2 + 2n + 1 - (n + 1)$ | *here the two (n+1)s have been multiplied* |
| $= n^2 + 2n + 1 - n - 1$ | *now the final (n + 1) has been 'opened up': – (n + 1) becomes –n – 1* |
| $= n^2 + n$ | *tidying up the expression, we find it ends up the same as the right-hand side of the original equation!* |

## Handling messy numbers

When you can use a calculator, it doesn't matter if the numbers you want to work with are large or awkward: you can tackle real-life problems, not just ones that have been tidied up to make them easier.

Here are a few examples of problems involving messy numbers.

- How many days (or hours, or minutes) have you been alive? When will your next 'round number' be?
- How many lines (or words, or letters) are there in the last book you read?
- What is the combined weight (or height, or age, or pocket money) of your whole class? or the whole school?

**Make up some 'messy number' questions that would be appropriate for children in your class.**
**What questions might the children come up with?**

Although the kinds of questions given here can be intriguing, the real power is being able to work with any numbers that arise in practical or real-life situations. In Section B there are several examples of situations where children can do this.

## *Trial and improvement*

Here are two examples of problems which can be solved using a trial and improvement approach. It is easy to assume that using a calculator means you use mental arithmetic less: these activities may surprise you in terms of the mathematical thinking they require.

---

### Targeting 100
- - - - - - - - - - - - - - - - - - -

Using only numbers and the ☒ and ☰ keys, find a number you can multiply 43 by to get 100.

- What mathematical ideas have you used?
- Can you think of a different strategy to reach the target?

---

**Invent some other challenges like this to try yourself, or to offer your class. What target numbers would be most appropriate?**

If you enjoy this kind of problem solving, here is a more difficult challenge. As you work on it, think about other similar problems that you and your class might pose for each other.

---

### Number detectives
- - - - - - - - - - - - - - - - - - - - - - - - -

They were a tricky pair to track down ... I didn't have much to go on.

Add them and you get 10, multiply them and you get 20.

---

Using a trial and improvement approach with immediate feedback from the calculator helps to develop confidence and fluency with numbers. Activities like these are easy to get in to. It doesn't matter how far off your first guess is: you can use what you learn to move on.

## *The calculator as a teaching aid*

There are lots of calculator games and puzzles available which focus on particular areas of mathematics. These can be used to help children practise and consolidate new ideas. The following example can be adapted to give experience with different aspects of place value.

---

### Place Invaders

*A calculator game for two players*

The first player puts a two-digit number into the calculator. The second player must subtract a number so that the units digit disappears or becomes 0.

Now the first player must get rid of the tens digit in the same way.

- Try starting with a 3 digit number ... or 4 digits ... or more ...
- Try allowing addition as well as subtraction ...

*For an extra challenge, give your partner a number with one or two places of decimals.*

---

# HOW CALCULATORS BEHAVE

You are probably already aware that calculators do not always behave exactly as we expect them to do. This can be intriguing, or disconcerting, depending on your point of view! In the classroom, these quirks can present problems, particularly if you have not come across them before. However, if you are aware of what is happening, some of the problems can be transformed into teaching opportunities.

One of the common causes of confusion can be that different calculators give different answers to the same calculation. If you have the opportunity, try the activities in this section on more than one calculator, so that you get a sense of these differences.

The calculations in the following activities are presented just as you need to key them in. Press the calculator keys to match the symbols that are printed here, even if you think they look a bit odd!

## *Disappearing digits*

The first problem is a very simple one. Most adults would never notice it, but it can be disconcerting for young children. Watch the calculator display carefully.

3 + 5 =

What actually happened as you pressed the keys?

'In the Reception class, Rachel was using her calculator to work out 3 + 5, but she was puzzled by what happened. When she pressed +, nothing seemed to happen. Then she pressed 5 and the 3 disappeared! She was sure something had gone wrong, but her teacher encouraged her to carry on. She carefully pressed = and found that an 8 had appeared. It took her some time, exploring other examples, and going back to counting objects to check, before she accepted that 8 was the answer. She felt a bit cheated that the calculator didn't show her the whole calculation.'

This isn't a problem which is likely to worry children for long, but their reactions to the initial confusion may show up another of the calculator's quirks; this time one which can lead into some useful mathematical thinking.

Because what they expect doesn't happen, that is, the symbol doesn't appear on the display, children may try pressing the key again. So they may actually key in

3 + + 5 =

or

3 + 5 = =

Depending on the make of your calculator, one of these methods sets up a constant operation, which is repeated each time you press =. In the first case, this may repeatedly add 3, in the second it will add 5. If you go on pressing = you will get a sequence of numbers appearing: for example, 5 then 8 then 13 then 18 then 23, and so on. You may see a letter k (for constant!) appear on the display. You will need to experiment with your own calculator to see exactly how it works.

**Get your calculator to show the 6 times table, ... or multiples of 13, ... or the 7 times table backwards from 84.**

If the calculation involves more than two numbers, the calculator may have another surprise in store.

$3 + 5 + 7 =$

When the second + is pressed, you can see the effect. On my simple calculator, the 5 is replaced by 8: the calculator has worked out the first part of the calculation already.

**Does the same happen on all calculators? What happens if you use subtraction or multiplication instead of addition?**

## *Disappearing digits 2: the curse of the zeros*

$5.30 \times 7 =$

This kind of calculation might arise in problems involving money or measures. What result does the calculator actually show?

The disappearing zero can be disconcerting for children, particularly when they are thinking of their answer as an amount of money. There are opportunities here to reinforce understanding of place value, and the slightly different conventions we use when writing and reading currency values. If we think only about the numbers, 11.7 ('eleven point seven') is the same as 11.70 ('eleven point seven zero'). We write £11.70 but not £11.7, because we read this as 'eleven pounds seventy' not 'eleven pounds seven'. It isn't surprising that children become confused about how to interpret the values of decimals.

## *Funny numbers*

Children exploring a calculator will soon discover that they sometimes get numbers which are unfamiliar.

$5 - 12 =$

$12 \div 5 =$

You won't be surprised by the results that you get to either of these calculations, but children may well be. In the children's terms these are calculations that 'you can't do', or that 'don't go exactly', but the calculator doesn't know this.

Many young children don't distinguish clearly between $12 - 5$ and $5 - 12$, so they might easily key in the wrong calculation by mistake. Some children may enjoy trying to test the calculator by giving it problems they think are impossible.

'Amy and Leila thought it was very funny when their calculator got the answer to 5 − 12 wrong. "It says the answer is 7, but you can't do 5 − 12!" Then they noticed that 12 − 5 = 7, so they guessed that the calculator had turned the sum round. Their teacher asked about the line that had appeared on the calculator display in front of the 7. Up to this point the girls had just ignored this, but now they started to think about what it might mean.'

They experimented a bit more to see when it appeared. At first they thought that it was the calculator's way of saying that the sum couldn't be done, but they noticed that the numbers which appeared seemed to match doing the sum backwards. Their teacher encouraged them to share their problem with the rest of the class. In the discussion, some children remembered seeing numbers written like this, and thought they might mean less than zero. The teacher was able to use a number line to offer them an image of these new and mysterious numbers.

A little later, the class were working on different ways of making 20. Leila offered "minus one add 21".'

There are lots of occasions when children will get decimals in an answer given by the calculator. This could be a good opportunity to start talking about extending place value, but younger children will probably be happy with the explanation that when they get 2.4 as the answer to 12 ÷ 5, it means 'two and a bit'. Similarly children may want to use familiar fractions in working with calculators, and will be happy to accept that .5 is the way the calculator writes a half.

## *A mind of its own?*

Try this calculation on your calculator just as it is written here.

3 + 5 × 7 =

What answer did you get? What answer did you *expect*? If you try the same sequence on a different calculator, do you get the same answer?

The problem is that the original calculation is ambiguous. It could mean 'add three and five, and then multiply by seven', or 'add five times seven on to three'. My simple calculator worked out the first of these, and gave me the answer 56. (When I pressed '×', 8 appeared on the display.) However, my scientific calculator chose to give me the answer 38. This time, when I pressed '×', nothing changed.

Mathematicians used a convention to decide how to deal with an ambiguous calculation like this. You might remember learning it as BODMAS. This defines an order in which the operations are to be used. The DMAS stands for Division, Multiplication, Addition, Subtraction, and the scientific calculator has been programmed to follow this convention, so when it is given $\times$ or $\div$ in a sequence of instructions, it is alerted to work out these operations before + or −.

People can use common sense and knowledge of the context to decide what to do, but the calculator can't. Normally, if we want to make the calculation unambiguous, we need to add brackets (that's what the B stands for: the O could be 'of', but I think it is really there to make a word that can be pronounced!). So we would write $(3 + 5) \times 7$, or $3 + (5 \times 7)$. More sophisticated calculators may have brackets, which could be used in this situation: simple calculators just carry out the operations in the order they are entered. So if I want to work out $3 + (5 \times 7)$ on my simple calculator, I need to turn the sequence around and key in

$5 \times 7 + 3 =$

You might be feeling a bit confused by all this detail, but it is worth sticking with it, and getting the ideas clear for yourself. Thinking about what the calculator is doing can provide a really powerful way for children to gain more insight into the structure of arithmetic, and the conventions that are used. This sort of understanding will increase their fluency in arithmetic, and is an invaluable foundation for manipulating algebra.

**Explore some other examples until you feel confident about how the calculator will behave.**

## *Return of the disappearing digits*

The final example of the calculator's behaviour in this section also shows itself most clearly if you use different kinds of calculators.

$10 \div 3 \times 3 =$

When I tried this, my simple calculator gave 9.9999999, while the scientific calculator gave 10. The explanation is fairly simple. When the calculator works out $10 \div 3$, the result isn't exactly 3.3333333, but this is what it shows. The real result has an infinite number of threes after the decimal point, but the calculator can only show seven of these, and it only *remembers* one or two more digits than it displays. So in the second part of the calculation it is actually working out 3.333333333 × 3, and that is how it gets its result.

The scientific calculator also shows 3.3333333 at the half-way point in the sequence, but it has a more efficient memory, and retains the *calculation* as well as the result. It is programmed so that multiplication 'undoes' division, and so it gives a result of 10.

# THOSE OTHER KEYS

Even the simplest calculators have a few other keys in addition to those for numbers and the four basic operations. There are generally four keys for operating the calculator's memory.

**M+** can be used to add whatever number is currently displayed to the memory. A letter M will usually appear on the display to indicate that there is a number being held. Similarly **M–** will subtract the number on display from the total being held in memory. You can recall the number in the memory using **MR**, and then operate on it like any other number. **MC** clears the memory.

The use of the square root key √ is straightforward: it gives the square root of whatever number it follows.

The percentage key % is the one which causes most confusion, and unfortunately different makes of calculator operate in different ways. You will need to experiment with your calculator, or look back at the instructions which came with it, to see exactly what it does.

On many calculators, the per cent key is designed to work out percentage increases or decreases which are often used in commerce. To see how your calculator works, try this example. To work out what you would pay for something costing £38 plus VAT, press the keys as follows.

38 + 17.5 %

You will probably get the answer 44.65. (If you don't, then your calculator is using a different method, which is described later.) Now work out what you would pay if the shop is also offering a 25% discount, by pressing

44.65 – 25 %

(You might like to think about whether you would get a better bargain by taking the discount off first before you add on the VAT.)

The per cent key compresses the calculation that you might otherwise do to add or subtract a percentage. For example, I might add VAT like this:

38 × .175 = 6.65     38 + 6.65 = 44.65

or like this

38 × 1.175 = 44.65

When you tried the original calculation, you may have got the answer 46.06. What the calculator has done here is to increase £38 by an amount which is 17.5% of the final figure. This may seem a strange calculation to make: it seems to be based on the notion of calculating profits. It assumes that I want to know how much to sell an item for in order to make that percentage profit. So, in the example we tried, if I had bought an item for £38, and I sell it for £46.06, I would have made 17.5% of the selling price as a profit. You may well decide that this is not a very useful facility – either for your own use, or for the classroom!

# Different calculators

In this chapter we have already mentioned two different kinds of calculators, which have been labelled 'simple' and 'scientific', but in fact there is a bewildering array of different calculators now available. In some cases it may be hard to distinguish between them, but some do offer significantly different features. Calculator enthusiasts will want to know much more detail than it would be appropriate to give here, but for most people a few broad categories will be sufficient.

The simple *four-function calculator* is the one we are most familiar with, and which is generally most appropriate for use in primary schools. It performs the four functions of addition, subtraction, multiplication and division, as well as keys for per cent, square root and for controlling the memory (as described above).

There is a whole range of *scientific calculators* with many more keys. The exact functions of these vary, but typically they offer statistical and trigonometric functions, and have long since replaced the books of four-figure tables which used to be common in secondary schools.

*Graphical calculators* are easily recognised by their larger display screens. These calculators can be used to plot graphs of mathematical functions, as well as to store and graph simple numerical data. These calculators are really aimed more at secondary pupils, though they may have some potential at the top of Key Stage 2. One advantage they do have for younger children is that they display the whole calculation as well as the answer (see Rachel's problem described in 'How calculators behave'), though at present they are probably too expensive to use just for this reason!

More advanced still, we are now seeing a new range of hand-held machines which are perhaps more like small computers than calculators. The *TI 92* has just appeared on the market, and will surely soon be followed by others. This combines the functions of a graphical calculator with built-in software for dynamic geometry and algebraic manipulation which have previously only been available on computers. Again these are aimed at older pupils.

Other hand-held machines which are blurring the distinction between calculators and computers are the *palmtops* or *pocket books*. These are described in more detail in Chapter 7.

---

Activities in Section B which make use of calculators are:

**Chapter 8 Growing and shrinking**
  Scaling models and pictures (Key Stage 2)
  Doubling and halving (Key Stage 1)

**Chapter 9 Exploring patterns**
  Number bonds (Key Stage 1)
  Multiplication tables (Key Stage 2)
  Number patterns (Key Stage 2)

# CHAPTER 2

# WORKING WITH A DATABASE

> The purpose of this chapter is
> * to show you some of the things you can do with a database;
> * to help you make a start with using a database yourself.

You will get most out of this chapter if you can use a database to try out some of the activities and challenges – and even more if you can work on them with a colleague. It doesn't matter which software you use: all databases have similar features, but it would be useful to have the handbook for the one you are using so that you can check exactly what to do. If you can't find the handbook, it is still worth having a go. You can probably work out what to do from the information given on the screen.

## WHAT IS A DATABASE?

A database is a piece of software for storing information. The term **database** can be used both for the piece of software into which you can enter data, and for a collection of data which has already been stored. So, for example, within school you might have one or more database packages or programs (such as *Junior Database*, or *Pin Point*), but you may also have a database of children's records in the school office. This can be a bit confusing to start with, so in this chapter 'database' will be used to mean the software, and collections of data will be referred to in other ways.

In a number of ways, databases are similar to spreadsheets, which are discussed in Chapter 3. They offer many of the same features, but while spreadsheets are generally more useful for dealing with numerical information, databases offer more possibilities if you want to store and handle verbal information.

Within a database, information can be entered as separate **records**. You might find it helpful to relate this to the sort of card index which used to be common in libraries. Each record is like a separate card. On each record you can put a number of pieces of information, known as **fields**. In the library, these fields might be the title, author's name, publisher, date of publication, and so on.

The advantage of storing this information on a computer, rather than in a card index, is that it is easy to find records based on any of these fields. In the card index, the cards have to be filed in a particular order; say by the book title. If I want to find other books by the same author, I would need to go to a separate index, where a duplicate set of cards are stored in a different order. Once the information is stored on a computer, I can easily **sort** the data into order based on any of the fields, or I can **search** for all the records containing the data I am interested in. So I could search for all the books by a particular author, or all the books published in a particular year, or all the books with 'blue' in the title. I can even search for combinations, such as all the books published by Penguin, before 1950, by authors with the initials 'M. L.'.

# STORING INFORMATION

If you haven't used a database before, it would be worth spending a bit of time trying to store some information yourself before reading on. Choose some collection of information that you can get access to easily, and which it might be useful to organise in some way. I am going to use an address book for the examples in this section, but you could work on the video tapes piled up on the shelf above the television, the audio tapes you use in school, your favourite recipes, etc.

First of all, you need to set up the **fields** you are going to use for each record, and use these to create a sort of template for entering the information. You can generally make some choices about the **layout** of the records, by deciding where you want each field on the page, and how much space it will take up.

 **Open up your database and find out how to create fields on a new record. You may need to use the handbook to help you.**

As this is just an experiment, don't try to create too many fields. Entering information can get very tedious, and a few examples will be enough to get a sense of what is possible. The software you are using may require you to say in advance how many **records** or **fields** you want to make. If so, ask for more than you think you will need: you will almost certainly change your mind!

You may also need to specify what type of information the field will contain. This may be **text** (sometimes called 'alphanumeric'), **numbers**, or possibly a **date**. The software will treat these types of information in different ways. Combinations of numbers and letters (such as 30 cm, or 5 secs.) will be treated as words. Some databases will also allow you to create fields which carry out a **calculation**. For example, if the database was used to store census data which contained the date of birth, a calculation could be put in a field to work out each person's age when the census was taken.

Figure 2 shows how I have decided to organise the information in my 'address book' database.

```
Surname:

First name:

Address:              Birthday:

Town:
                      Phone:
County:

Postcode:
```

FIGURE 2

I have separated out each piece of information so that I have as many options as possible when I want to look up some information. For example, I might want to check which of my family and friends has a birthday this month, or look up the name of that couple I met on holiday three years ago who live in Crewe.

I have decided to make a separate record for each person, so I will need to duplicate much of the information for members of the same family. It would be tedious to do this in an ordinary address book, but on the computer it is easy to make a copy of a record, and then alter it in some way before saving it as a new item in the database.

One reason for making separate records for individuals is that I want to store information about business as well as home addresses. In fact, my first attempt at creating the record won't really cope with this, so I need to make some changes and add some extra fields. I'm going to add new fields to make it clear whether it is a home or a work address, and also for fax and electronic mail numbers. I may not have all of these pieces of information for all the people in my address book, but it won't matter if I leave some of the fields blank. Once I have saved this design for my record, I am now ready to start entering information about some of my friends (figure 3).

| | |
|---|---|
| **Surname:** | **Work/Home:** |
| **First name:** | |
| **Address:** | **Birthday:** |
| **Town:** | |
| | **Phone:** |
| **County:** | **Fax:** |
| **Postcode:** | |
| | **email:** |

FIGURE 3

 **Once you have decided on your fields and planned the layout, enter information for a few of your records.**

## ACCESSING INFORMATION

Databases vary in the facilities they provide, but there are two basic ways in which information can always be accessed. These are **sorting** the records into order, and **searching** for a particular record or group of records. When the records have been manipulated in some way they can be **displayed** on the screen, **printed** or **saved** in a new file.

### Sorting

I might decide to **sort** my address book into alphabetical order of *surname* so that I can print out a list. As it contains several records for people with the same surname, I may need to specify that the second field to be used for this sorting is *firstname*. That would put *Ann Smith* before *John Smith*, but after *Alan Smith*.

### Searching

If I decide that I want to separate out the business addresses I have stored, I would need to **search** for all those records which have 'Work' in the *Work/Home* field. Sometimes the search might be much more complicated than this, based on two or three different fields. Some software allows you to do this in one operation; in other cases the search may have to be done in stages.

Use the records you have stored to experiment with sorting and searching your information. You may need to use the handbook to help you.
Find out how to print out and save records.

# GRAPHING

Many databases, particularly those designed for use in schools, offer facilities for drawing graphs. Databases designed for commercial use may not offer graphing directly, but you may be able to transfer data to a spreadsheet in order to draw graphs.

You will need to specify which fields are to be graphed, and then choose from a range of graphs which will be the most appropriate. Many of the comments on graphing from spreadsheets in the section 'Working with graphs' in Chapter 3 apply equally to databases. Graphs can be produced at any stage, so graphical representation may be more effective after the data has been sorted or selected in some way.

 Use your handbook to help you explore how to produce graphs in your database, and look ahead to Chapter 3 for some more ideas.

---

Classroom activities using databases described in Section B are:

**Chapter 7 Ourselves**
Body measures (Key Stage 1 and Key Stage 2)
... and other data (Key Stage 1 and Key Stage 2)
Ourselves and other people (Key Stage 2)
Our clothes (Key Stage 2)

**Chapter 10 Vehicles**
Testing toy vehicles  (Key Stage 1 and Key Stage 2)
Designing and making vehicles (Key Stage 1 and Key Stage 2)
Paper helicopters (Key Stage 2)

**CHAPTER 3**

# WORKING WITH A SPREADSHEET

---

> The purpose of this chapter is
> - to show you some of the things you can do with a spreadsheet;
> - to help you make a start with using a spreadsheet yourself.

You will get most out of this chapter if you can use a spreadsheet to try out some of the activities and challenges – and even more if you can work on them with a colleague. It doesn't matter which software you use: all spreadsheets have similar features, but it would be useful to have the handbook for the one you are using so that you can check exactly what to do. If you can't find the handbook, it is still worth having a go. You can probably work out what to do from the information given on the screen.

## WHAT IS A SPREADSHEET?

The word spreadsheet originated in book-keeping, where it simply means a large sheet of paper, ruled in rows and columns, on which information, numbers and calculations can be laid out.

On a computer, a spreadsheet is a piece of software which gives you a screen version of such a sheet, set out in rows (which are labelled with numbers) and columns (labelled with letters). When you first start up the software you will be looking at the top left-hand corner of the sheet, which will look something like figure 4.

|   | A | B | C | D | E |
|---|---|---|---|---|---|
| 1 |   |   |   |   |   |
| 2 |   |   |   |   |   |
| 3 |   |   |   |   |   |
| 4 |   |   |   |   |   |
| 5 |   |   |   |   |   |

FIGURE 4

The number of rows and columns you can see will vary according to which software you are using, but the computer is actually 'remembering' a much larger sheet.

The individual boxes on the spreadsheet are often called **cells**. Each cell has its own name, given by its column and row labels, e.g. A1, G17, M8. In the spreadsheet shown here cell A2 is highlighted.

# GETTING ORGANISED

If you aren't familiar with using a spreadsheet, the activities in this section will help you to get started.

**Open up your spreadsheet and see what it looks like.**

You can 'talk to' a particular cell by pointing and clicking with a mouse, or by using the cursor (arrow) keys. You can also move around the sheet, and see different parts of it.

**Find your way around. How many rows and columns does your spreadsheet have?**

When a cell is **highlighted**, you can type information into it. What you type might be words or numbers, so a spreadsheet can be useful for organising and setting out information that you want to have in columns or as a table. For example, you might use a spreadsheet to set out your weekly timetable, to keep a class list and record activities children have completed, or even to make a shopping list.

**Use your spreadsheet to set out your weekly timetable, or some other information you need to organise.**

It may be a bit more difficult than you expected to decide on the best way to set the information out. You may find you need to change the **column width** or the **row height**, or even to **insert** extra rows or columns.

You may also be able to **format** the cells in other ways, changing the **font** that is used in them, making the writing bold or italic, or even changing the colour or putting a **border** around the cell.

When you are happy with what you have done, you will be able to **save** it, or to **print** it out. If you cannot see how to do this from the menus on the screen, you will need to look it up in your handbook.

## *Letting the spreadsheet do the work*

You can put instructions to carry out a calculation into a cell, using a **function** or a **formula**. So, if you recorded the money collected from a sponsored walk, as in figure 5, you could set up the spreadsheet to work out the total. The total would be updated as you typed in the amounts collected by the remaining children.

|  | A | B | C | D |
|---|---|---|---|---|
| 1 | Name | Amount collected |  |  |
| 2 |  | in £ |  |  |
| 3 | Sarah | 3.57 |  |  |
| 4 | Andreas | 4.10 |  |  |
| 5 | Jodie | 5.00 |  |  |
| 6 | Sam | 3.85 |  |  |
| 7 | Nita | 2.16 |  |  |
| 8 | Peter |  |  |  |
| 9 | Amy |  |  |  |
| 10 |  |  |  |  |
| 11 |  |  | Total in £ | 18.68 |

FIGURE 5

Notice that the pounds sign is in the column heading, not in the cells that contain the amounts. The spreadsheet will treat words and numbers differently: it will only allow you to do calculations with numbers. With some spreadsheets you may need to tell the computer whether you are going to enter a word or a number, but generally the software will recognise which it is. If you put in a combination of numbers and other symbols, such as 42 cm, £5, or 10:30 a.m., the spreadsheet will treat this as a word.

### USING A FORMULA

Once you feel at home with your spreadsheet, you are ready to use it for some mathematics. The only technical information you need is how to put a **formula** into a cell. On many spreadsheets you do this by typing '=' followed by the calculation you want to do, but some software may have other ways of telling the spreadsheet to expect a formula.

In figure 6, there is a formula in cell C4, which adds the number in A1 to the number in B2. The sheet on the left shows the result, and the one on the right the formula. Normally the spreadsheet will show only the result, but it may be possible to show the formula if you want to.

|   | A | B | C |
|---|---|---|---|
| 1 | 25 |   |   |
| 2 |   | 17 |   |
| 3 |   |   |   |
| 4 |   |   | 42 |
| 5 |   |   |   |

|   | A | B | C |
|---|---|---|---|
| 1 | 25 |   |   |
| 2 |   | 17 |   |
| 3 |   |   |   |
| 4 |   |   | =A1+B2 |
| 5 |   |   |   |

This means
'add the number in A1 to the
number in B2'

FIGURE 6

You can type in any arithmetic instructions you like; A3 - 5, D7 * 2.5, (B10 *2) – 6. These instructions use the spreadsheet's special notation, which is a kind of algebra. The label for a cell is a way of referring to any number that might be put in the cell, so it is equivalent to using a letter like 'x' or 'n' to stand for a variable. You might think of the formula in a cell as being like the rule in a function machine. (Notice that, like many other computer applications, the spreadsheet uses * and / for multiplication and division.)

**Set up a spreadsheet with a number in one cell. Put a *secret* formula into another cell, and challenge a friend to work out what it is by changing the original number.**
**In another cell, put a formula that undoes the effect of the first one.**

If you can't find time with a colleague to work on this, you might still set yourself the challenge of working out a formula which undoes another one. Mathematically this second formula is the inverse of the first – in fact the two are inverses of each other. Another way to think about inverses is to think of those puzzles to find 'the number you first thought of'.

So, if the original formula is A1 + 3, you would need to take 3 off the result to get back to the original number. Figure 7 illustrates a few more examples:

|   | A | B | C | D |
|---|---|---|---|---|
| 1 | 34 | | 'doing' | 'undoing' |
| 2 | | | =A1÷9 | =C2×9 |
| 3 | | | | |
| 4 | | | =(A1×2)+5 | =(C4−5)÷2 |
| 5 | | | | |
| 6 | | | =(A1−10)×7 | =(C6÷7)+10 |
| 7 | | | | |
| 8 | | | | |

FIGURE 7

## USING FUNCTIONS

As well as typing in your own formulas, you can make use of **functions** that are programmed into the spreadsheet. For example, you can use a function to find the *total* or the *average* of a set of numbers. Usually you can put a function into a cell by pasting it from a list in one of the menus, or by typing in the name of the function, using = as you did for a formula. You also need to show which cells you want the function to apply to. For example

### = AVERAGE(D5:D18)

will give the (mean) average of all the cells from D5 to D18.

|   | A | B | C | D |
|---|---|---|---|---|
| 1 | Name | Amount collected | | |
| 2 | | in £ | | |
| 3 | Sarah | 3.57 | | |
| 4 | Andreas | 4.10 | | |
| 5 | Jodie | 5.00 | | |
| 6 | Sam | 3.85 | | |
| 7 | Nita | 2.16 | | |
| 8 | Peter | 0.94 | | |
| 9 | Amy | 1.55 | | |
| 10 | Ellie | 3.02 | | |
| 11 | Jo | 2.43 | | |
| 12 | Pani | 1.85 | | |
| 13 | | | | |
| 14 | | | Total in £ | |
| 15 | | | Average | |
| 16 | | | | |

FIGURE 8

Set up a spreadsheet like figure 8, giving amounts of money collected on a sponsored walk. Use functions to give the total amount collected, and the average collected per child.

You will find that there are lots of functions available on your spreadsheet, many of which may seem rather obscure! Don't worry. You will probably never need to use them, and you will soon get to know the ones that are useful for you.

## Using more power

If you want the spreadsheet to perform the same calculation over and over again, you can **fill down** or **fill right** with a formula or a function into other cells. (You can never work upwards, or right to left on a spreadsheet.) This is a very powerful idea, and once you have used it you will start to get a sense of the exciting things that you can do with this kind of software. Here are two examples of how you might use the idea of copying a formula.

### FUNCTION MACHINES

In the challenge above, the spreadsheet was used rather like a function machine, with a starting (input) number, and a rule which gave a result (output). If you wanted to try different inputs, you had to change the starting number, so you couldn't see all the numbers you had tried at once. This makes it harder to guess what the rule is. If you want to be able to see all the inputs and their corresponding outputs, you could set up the spreadsheet differently (figure 9).

| | A | B |
|---|---|---|
| **1** | Input | Output |
| **2** | 5 | =A2×4+1 |
| **3** | 2 | =A3×4+1 |
| **4** | 10 | =A4×4+1 |
| **5** | | =A5×4+1 |
| **6** | | =A6×4+1 |
| **7** | | =A7×4+1 |
| **8** | | =A8×4+1 |
| **9** | | =A9×4+1 |
| **10** | | =A10×4+1 |
| **11** | | =A11×4+1 |
| **12** | | =A12×4+1 |

What has been copied is not

*'multiply the number in A2 by four and add one'*

but

*'multiply the number in the cell on the left by four and add one'*

FIGURE 9

Cell A2 contains the first input number, and cell B2 contains the formula =A2*4 + 1, so what you would normally see in this cell is the result, 21. This formula has then been filled down column B. Notice how the formula changes in each row. As other inputs are typed into cells in column A, the outputs will appear in column B.

In order to fill down, you need to tell the computer which cell the formula is in, and which cells you want to fill. Usually you do this by highlighting, beginning at the cell containing the formula, but some software may use different methods.

### NUMBER PATTERNS

Another example of the power of copying a formula is to produce a simple number pattern. The number pattern in the spreadsheet in figure 10 was produced by typing 1 into cell A2, putting the formula = A2 + 2 into cell B2, and then filling along row B.

|   | A | B | C | D | E | F | G | H |
|---|---|---|---|---|---|---|---|---|
| 1 |   |   |   |   |   |   |   |   |
| 2 | 1 | 3 | 5 | 7 | 9 | 11 | 13 | 15 |

Changing this number will create different patterns

FIGURE 10

**CHALLENGE!**

**Use your spreadsheet to produce some number patterns. Can you make a row of odd numbers? or multiples of 5? How about counting backwards in threes?**

# WORKING WITH GRAPHS

The ability to produce graphs from your data is another powerful feature of spreadsheets. In some spreadsheets graphs are referred to as **charts**. Before you draw a graph, you will need to highlight the data that you want to graph, and you will then probably be offered a choice of the kinds of graph you can produce.

You can choose the most appropriate graph to represent the data you are working with.  If you wanted a visual image of the amounts of money collected in the sponsored walk we looked at earlier, it would probably be best to use a bar chart (figure 11).

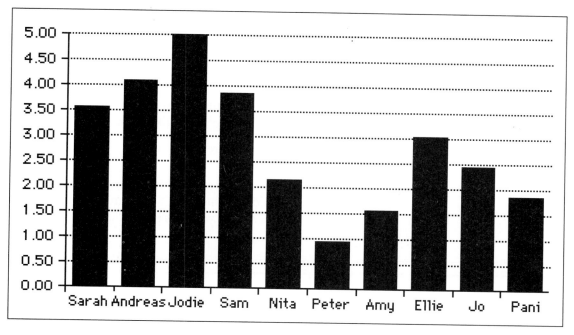

FIGURE 11

But you might feel you get a better picture if you put the data into order first. Again you will need to highlight the data you want to **sort**, and then use the menus to help you. You will need to make clear which column you want your sorting to be based on. In figure 12, the data was sorted on column B.

|    | A       | B       |
|----|---------|---------|
| 1  | Name    | Amount  |
| 2  |         | in £    |
| 3  | Peter   | 0.94    |
| 4  | Amy     | 1.55    |
| 5  | Pani    | 1.85    |
| 6  | Nita    | 2.16    |
| 7  | Jo      | 2.43    |
| 8  | Ellie   | 3.02    |
| 9  | Sarah   | 3.57    |
| 10 | Sam     | 3.85    |
| 11 | Andreas | 4.10    |
| 12 | Jodie   | 5.00    |
| 13 |         |         |

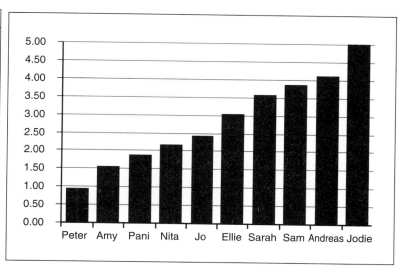

FIGURE 12

If I had sorted on column A, the spreadsheet would have arranged the data in alphabetical order.

**Find out how to make a graph from data on your spreadsheet. Notice that when you have made a graph, you can probably alter its appearance in a number of ways. Try changing the size of the graph, and see what happens to the scales shown on the axes. Sort the data, and see how your graph looks now.**

## Other kinds of graphs

One of the beauties of a spreadsheet is that many different kinds of graphs can be produced very quickly. Sometimes choosing a different kind of graph can help you represent data more clearly. Here are some examples.

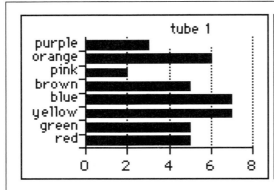

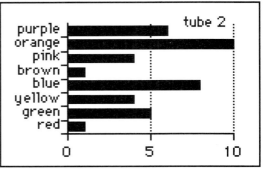

|    | A      | B      | C      | D      |
|----|--------|--------|--------|--------|
| 1  |        | tube 1 |        | tube 2 |
| 2  | red    | 5      | red    | 1      |
| 3  | green  | 5      | green  | 5      |
| 4  | yellow | 7      | yellow | 4      |
| 5  | blue   | 7      | blue   | 8      |
| 6  | brown  | 5      | brown  | 1      |
| 7  | pink   | 2      | pink   | 4      |
| 8  | orange | 6      | orange | 10     |
| 9  | purple | 3      | purple | 6      |
| 10 |        |        |        |        |

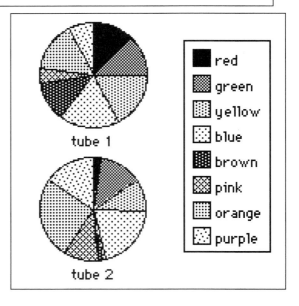

FIGURE 13

In an investigation about the mixture of colours in tubes of Smarties, children might record the results from several different tubes (figure 13). These results could be shown in bar charts, but pie charts might show up the differences more clearly.

On the spreadsheet, the column showing the colours of Smarties has been copied so that it is next to each column showing the numbers of those colours in the tube. This is because on most spreadsheets you cannot draw a graph using two columns unless they are next to each other.

After collecting data about their body measurements, children might use scatter graphs to investigate questions such as whether taller children have bigger feet (figure 14).

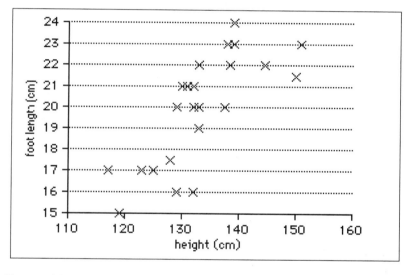

FIGURE 14

This graph indicates that there is some link between height and foot length, since the crosses do form a broad band diagonally across the graph. The empty areas in the top left and bottom right corners of the graph indicate that there were no short children with very big feet, and no tall children with very small feet.

If you are exploring number patterns, such as the square numbers, then looking at line graphs might give some new insights (figure 15).

|   | A | B |
|---|---|---|
| 1 | Counting | Square |
| 2 | 1 | 1 |
| 3 | 2 | 4 |
| 4 | 3 | 9 |
| 5 | 4 | 16 |
| 6 | 5 | 25 |
| 7 | 6 | 36 |
| 8 | 7 | 49 |
| 9 | 8 | 64 |
| 10 | 9 | 81 |
| 11 | 10 | 100 |
| 12 | 11 | 121 |
| 13 | 12 | 144 |
| 14 | 13 | 169 |
| 15 | 14 | 196 |
| 16 | 15 | 225 |
| 17 | 16 | 256 |
| 18 | 17 | 289 |
| 19 | 18 | 324 |
| 20 | 19 | 361 |
| 21 | 20 | 400 |

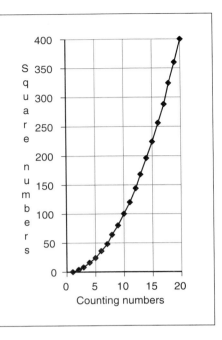

FIGURE 15

Classroom activities using spreadsheets described in Section B are:

**Chapter 7 Ourselves**
    Body measures (Key Stage 1 and Key Stage 2)
    ...and other data (Key Stage 1 and Key Stage 2)
    How we grow (Key Stage 1 and Key Stage 2)
    Ourselves and other people (Key Stage 2)
    Our clothes (Key Stage 2)

**Chapter 8 Growing and shrinking**
    Giants (Key Stage 1 and Key Stage 2)
    Scaling models and pictures (Key Stage 2)
    Doubling and halving (Key Stage 1 and Key Stage 2)
    Large and small numbers (Key Stage 1 and Key Stage 2)
    Wheels (Key Stage 2)

**Chapter 9 Exploring patterns**
    Number bonds (Key Stage 1)
    Multiplication tables (Key Stage 2)
    Number patterns (Key Stage 2)
    Patterns in chance (Key Stage 2)

Classroom activities using spreadsheets described in
Section B cont.:

**Chapter 10 Vehicles**
Testing toy vehicles (Key Stage 1 and Key Stage 2)
Designing and making vehicles (Key Stage 1 and Key Stage 2)
Paper helicopters (Key Stage 2)

# CHAPTER 4

# WORKING WITH LOGO

The purpose of this chapter is
- to give you a brief introduction to using Logo to draw with the turtle;
- to show you some of the other things you can do with Logo which may be of mathematical interest;
- to help you make a start with using Logo yourself.

You will get most out of this chapter if you can use Logo to try out some of the activities and challenges – and even more if you can work on them with a colleague. It doesn't matter which software you use: all versions of Logo have similar features, but it would be useful to have the handbook for the version you are using so that you can check exactly what to do. If you can't find the handbook, it is still worth having a go, though you may find that you will need to try several ways of doing some things, or better still, find someone who can help you!

However, this chapter doesn't set out to describe *everything* that you can do with Logo – that would take a whole book, and there are several good ones around already (some of which are listed in the Further Reading section at the end of this book). The ideas here are ones which are appropriate for mathematical work at primary school level – but once you have tried them you may well want to explore further, and your children certainly will!

## WHAT IS LOGO?

Logo is a programming language which has been specially written so that it can be learned and used in an easy and natural way. Although it is very powerful, and can be used for very complex and sophisticated programming, it has a very easy and inviting starting point, through controlling a 'turtle'. The turtle can be made to move around using simple commands: **forward, back, left, right**. As it moves, the turtle can draw a line to show its path.

There are a number of different versions of Logo available which are frequently found in schools. Probably the most popular are the versions produced by *Logotron* for BBC and Archimedes machines, and by RM for Nimbus machines. There are also several versions which run on Apple and PC machines, of which *LogoWriter* is becoming very popular. A number of software packages have been produced which are Logo–like, and provide some of the features of Logo, particularly for turtle graphics. Finally there are a number of robots like *Roamer, Pip* and *Pixie* which move around independently, controlled by Logo–like commands. These form a very good introduction to Logo, and can be made to carry pens so that they can be used for drawing. However, their accuracy is dependent on the surface they are running on.

Logo commands can often be abbreviated (**fd, bk, rt, lt** are generally accepted, although some software may use different conventions). Each of these commands needs to be followed by a number, to tell the turtle how far to move or turn. The screen turtle moves in *turtle steps*, which are very small, so commands like **fd 100** or **bk 70** are appropriate. This can provide a valuable opportunity for children to work with larger numbers. Programmable robots like *Roamer, Pip* and *Pixie* have control pads which include direction arrows. They generally move in units which are equivalent to their own length. *Roamer* and *Pip* have number pads to enter distances. *Pixie*, a smaller robot designed for use by very young children, uses the convention of repeated presses on the direction arrow: pressing the forward arrow three times moves *Pixie* forward three times its own length. Directions for turning also have to include a number to indicate the size of the turn. *Pixie* turns 90 degrees each time the right or left arrow is pressed (though this can be changed). *Roamer, Pip* and the screen turtle turn in degrees.

 **Load Logo, or get out a robot, and make yourself familiar with how to make it move and turn.**

If you are working with Logo on the screen, you will quickly need a few other commands to keep control of your drawing. Notice that these commands don't need to be followed by a number.

    **cs**   *clear screen*   or   **cg**   *clear graphics*

are useful when you want to start again. You can get the turtle back to its starting place by using **home**.

(It is impossible to give all the possible variations in commands, but the most common are given here, and your handbook, or a friendly colleague, will help you if your version of Logo uses different conventions.)

There is also a range of commands for controlling the pen. Some you might want to experiment with are:

| | | | |
|---|---|---|---|
| **pu** | *pen up* | **pe** | *pen erase* |
| **pd** | *pen down* | **setpc** | *set pen colour (plus a number to select the colour)* |

**Make a drawing with the turtle. Choose anything you want – but don't be afraid to adapt your ideas as you work!**
**If you have a printer available, find out how to print your picture.**

## GETTING MORE CONTROL

While you are drawing with the turtle, you are working at what is known as 'direct drive' on the drawing screen. All this means is that the computer carries out each command as you type it, and then forgets about it. This is fine to begin with, but as soon as you want to do anything more complicated it is much more efficient to teach the computer to remember the instructions you have given, so that you can reuse them, or go back to them to make changes. This is what is meant by programming the computer.

In Logo, you can teach the computer to carry out a series of commands (known as a procedure) by using the **editor**. This is a different screen within the software which allows you to type lists of commands which the computer will then store. (In some versions of Logo such as *LogoWriter*, the editor is known as the **flipside**.) Each list of commands is given a **title**. When this word is typed in, the whole list of commands will be carried out.

The details of how you move from the normal drawing screen to the editor, and back again vary in different versions of Logo. You will need to check with your own handbook for this, and also for the exact layout needed for procedures. On the next page is an example of a procedure to draw a shape. What do you think it will draw?

**Type either procedure into the editor. (Notice that you can give procedures almost any name you want.) Then go back to the drawing screen, type the name you have used for the title, and see if your prediction was correct.**
**Now go back to the editor and change splodge to draw larger or smaller shapes, or ones with more 'spokes', or ....**

**Procedure 1**          **Procedure 2**

```
to splodge
fd 85
bk 85
rt 90                    This procedure should
fd 85                    produce the same drawing
bk 85                    as splodge, but the
rt 90                    instructions have been
fd 85                    shortened by using repeat.
bk 85
rt 90
fd 85                    to quicksplodge
bk 85                    repeat 4 [fd 85 bk 85 rt 90]
rt 90                    end
end
```

An important point about procedures is that they can be **saved** and reloaded when you want to continue your work. In some versions of Logo, pictures drawn in direct drive cannot be saved.

**Find out how to save Logo work, and get it back.**

Once you have taught the computer to carry out a procedure, you can use it like any other command, even inside another procedure. For example, if I wanted to draw a row of splodges (figure 16), I might make a procedure like this:

```
to row
repeat 5 [splodge move]
end
```

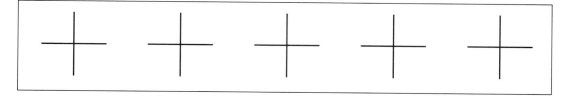

FIGURE 16

Of course, I would also need to write the procedure called **move** to get the turtle into the right place to draw the next splodge in the row. It might look like this.

```
to move
pu
rt 90 fd 200 lt 90
pd
end
```

# MAKING CHANGES

It is quite easy to draw splodges of different sizes by going back to the editor, and altering the number of turtle steps the turtle goes forward and back. However, this is rather time consuming, and if you want to be more in control you can change the size in a different way.

Instead of writing a procedure like splodge with a fixed size for the 'spokes', you can use a **variable**. This just means using a word or letter in place of the number of steps forward and back, so that you can tell the turtle each time how long you want the spokes to be. In most versions of Logo, this is how you would need to re-write the procedure:

```
to splodge :size
repeat 4 [fd :size bk :size rt 90]
end
```

**:size** tells the computer to look for a number. You might read it as 'the value of size'. (As with procedure names, I could have used any name, or even a single letter for the variable.) When you want to use splodge, you would now have to include a number for the size you want, e.g. splodge 100, splodge 33.

**Change your procedure to include a variable, and then draw splodges of different sizes.**

**If you are bored with splodges, try writing a procedure for different sized squares, or triangles, or circles, or ....**

# CONTROLLING HOW THE TURTLE MOVES

Once you know how to write procedures that use variables, it is fairly simple to write procedures to alter the turtle's movement in order to make things easier for children, or to create different effects on the screen.

## *Bigger steps*

For very young children, or those with limited number skills, the size of turtle steps may initially cause problems. If children find using large numbers a barrier, then it is possible to write short procedures to make the turtle move or turn in larger steps. Children could use the procedures **f** and **r** shown below instead of **fd** and **rt.**

```
to f :step              to r :turn
fd :step * 10           rt :turn * 45
end                     end
```

**f 6** will move the turtle forward 60 (i.e. 6 x 10).
**r 2** will turn the turtle right 90 degrees (i.e. 2 x 45).

These can obviously be adapted as appropriate, and similar procedures written for moving back and turning left. Children can use these initially, but the regular commands will still be available when they need them. You can save your set of procedures so that they can be loaded whenever they are needed.

## *Slowing down*

The screen turtle actually moves very fast: often so fast that you don't see the movement at all! This can be confusing for beginners, and unsatisfactory if you want to create an animated scene with the turtle moving around on a background design. Some versions of Logo allow you to change the turtle's speed using **slowturtle** and **fastturtle**, but these only give limited control.

It is possible to make your own procedure to slow the turtle down by using the command **wait** (or **pause**), which will make the turtle stop for a given time, usually in tenths of seconds. The trick is to get the turtle to move a bit, and then wait, over and over again. The procedure below gives the general pattern:

```
to dawdle
repeat 50 [fd 1 wait 1]
end
```

**Use this basic procedure to slow down your turtle. You can alter the numbers to change the way it appears to move.**

If you want to be able to choose how far the turtle moves, you will have to include a variable, for example:

```
to dawdle :distance
repeat :distance [fd 1 wait 1]
end
```

**It would be really smart to be able to choose how far the turtle goes *and* how fast it goes. But it isn't easy!**

Making turtles move at different speeds is particularly effective in versions of Logo where it is possible to change the shape of the turtle. This means you could have a cat walking across the screen, or a car driving down a hill, or a football that has just been kicked. For an even more realistic effect, you could design two turtle shapes, and use them alternately to show movement, like the flapping bird in figure 17.

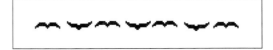

FIGURE 17

# USING CO-ORDINATES

As well as the normal drawing commands, it is possible to control the turtle's position by using co-ordinates. The Logo screen has an (invisible) co-ordinate grid, with the origin – the place where the axes cross – at the centre. Certain commands will return the turtle to the centre of the screen, but it can also be sent to different points on the screen by giving it X and Y co-ordinates. These are generally given using the commands **setx** and **sety**, followed by a number of turtle steps. A third command, **setpos**, followed by a list of two numbers inside brackets, allows you to set both co-ordinates at once.

Figure 18 shows the axes of the grid (which are normally invisible) and several turtles with the command which placed them where they are.

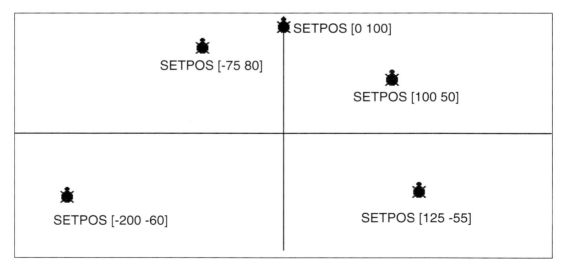

FIGURE 18

A technical note: the commands **setx, sety** and **setpos** may behave slightly differently in different versions of Logo. You will need to check whether the turtle normally draws when these commands are used. If it does, then you may want to lift the pen up before setting the turtle's position. These commands will always leave the turtle's heading (i.e. the direction in which it is facing) unchanged.

It is sometimes useful to set the turtle's heading to a particular direction, regardless of which way it was already facing. This can be done using **seth** (setheading), followed by the angle you require. This command uses bearings, as though the turtle were sitting at the centre of a 360 degree protractor. Positive bearings are measured clockwise from the 'north' line.

## *Where am I now?*

Occasionally it is useful to be able to find out the co-ordinates of the turtle's current position, perhaps because you want to return it to the same point. You can ask the turtle to tell you its position using **xcor, ycor** or **pos**. The turtle will also report its heading when you type **heading**. However, if you use these commands on their own, Logo will give you an **error message**, such as **I don't know what to do with 270**, because you have apparently entered a number without saying what to use it for. To avoid this, you could ask the computer to **print** (**pr**) or **show** the result.

# MORE TURTLES

In most versions of Logo, it is possible to work with more that one turtle.  You will need to check with your own handbook how many you have available: it should be at least 4, and may even be 32 or more!

However many there are, each has a number (you are generally working with turtle 0) and in some versions you can also give names to the turtles. In order to use more turtles, you need to talk to each one separately using the command **tell**. So you might **tell 2 fd 75** and **tell 0 bk 100 rt 90**. As soon as you name a turtle, you wake it up (or bring it into existence) and from then on it will be available. You will be talking to that turtle until you use **tell** again. You can talk to more than one turtle at a time by listing their numbers, e.g. **tell [1 3 0] fd 40**, and generally give an instruction to all of them by using **tell all**.

Working with multiple turtles takes a little getting used to, but it can be great fun for creating complex designs, and for making animated scenes. Once you have got the hang of remembering which turtle you are talking to, working with more turtles opens up many new possibilities.

# CALCULATING TURTLES

Logo has built into it the ability to do simple arithmetic, and also a number of more complex calculations, such as finding square roots and trigonometric functions. This opens up many more possibilities in addition to turtle graphics.

Calculations can be done on their own, or as a part of another instruction. (In fact we have already used some arithmetic in the procedures in Bigger steps, earlier in this chapter.) So, for example, you could type **fd 194 + 57** or **rt 360/7**. (As in many computer applications, * and / are use for multiplication and division.)

If you want to explore calculating in Logo separately from moving the turtle, you can simply type in the calculation, and press **return**. However, if you do this, Logo will give you an **error message** because you have apparently entered a number without a command. For example, if you type **37 * 117.5**, you will get a message something like **I don't know what to do with 4347.5**. To avoid this, and just get the answer, you could ask the computer to **print** the result, like this: **pr 37 * 117.5**. (See Where am I now?)

## *Function machines*

Including a calculation inside a procedure is a way of making a function machine. (Compare this to using a spreadsheet for the same activity, described in Chapter 3). As a classroom activity, it is a good way to play a 'guess my rule' game.

| | |
|---|---|
| One group of children write a short procedure to carry out some calculation on a variable. (Notice that they need to make the computer print the result, and use brackets to make their rule clear.) | to zap :number<br>pr (:number + 1) * 2<br>end |
| Other children now try to guess the rule by 'zapping' numbers until they can see a pattern. | **zap 2**   *gives*   6<br>**zap 6**   *gives*   14<br>**zap 0**   *gives*   2 |
| When they are ready to guess the rule, they can check either by looking in the editor, or better still by trying to write another procedure to **unzap.** | |

**Write a procedure that will square any number, or perhaps cube it. Or what about a procedure to add VAT to any price? Perhaps you could print out the original price, the VAT and the final price.**

## Again and again

Logo can be used to explore number patterns: you might like to compare this section to the activities using a spreadsheet described in Chapter 3.

In order to generate a number pattern, you need to write a procedure that does the same thing over and over again. The simplest way to do this is to use **tail recursion**. Don't be put off by the name: the idea is really very straightforward. Let's start with a procedure that will just print out the counting numbers.

| | |
|---|---|
| to snake :number | *(This snake is an adder!)* |
| pr :number | *This will print whatever number you start with.* |
| snake :number + 1 | *This line says 'Go back to the beginning, and do snake with that number plus one'.* |
| end | |

So, if you type **snake 3**, Logo will print ...

| | | |
|---|---|---|
| the original number | that is | **3** |
| the original number plus 1 | 3 + 1 | **4** |
| this new number plus 1 | 4 + 1 | **5** |
| this new number plus 1 | 5 + 1 | **6** |

... and so on. The only problem is, we haven't told it when to stop! If you typed in the procedure snake just as it is, you would need to press **escape** to stop the procedure, or it would go on printing numbers indefinitely.

To keep the procedure under control, we can tell it to stop when it gets to a certain number by adding a line to the procedure.

| | |
|---|---|
| to snake :number | |
| if :number = 10 [stop] | *This line will stop snake. What will be the largest number printed?* |
| pr :number | |
| snake :number + 1 | |
| end | |

**Write your own procedure like snake to print numbers up to 20, or going up in 2s, or down in 3s, or doubling, or ...**

Logo can be a powerful way of generating number patterns, and this can involve quite a lot of mathematical thinking. There are some ways in which this is quite a different activity from looking at number patterns with a calculator or with a spreadsheet. These different applications give different outputs, but also require different approaches from the user. When you have tried different methods yourself, you will be able to think about what children might gain from approaching number pattern activities in different ways. In mathematics, there are always different ways of approaching a particular task. Using a computer gives you the freedom to try many different approaches, and to decide which is best for you, and for the results you want to achieve. The 'best' way to do any piece of mathematics is the one with which you feel most comfortable, whether it is pencil and paper, Logo, a calculator, or matchsticks!

---

Classroom activities using Logo described in Section B are:

**Chapter 7 Ourselves**
    How we grow (Key Stage 1)

**Chapter 8 Growing and shrinking**
    Scaling pictures (Key Stage 1 and Key Stage 2)
    Large and small numbers (Key Stage 2)

**Chapter 9 Exploring patterns**
    Multiplication tables (Key Stage 2)
    Number patterns (Key Stage 1 and Key Stage 2)
    Designing wrapping paper (Key Stage 2)
    Patterns in chance (Key Stage 2)

**Chapter 10 Vehicles**
    Routes and directions  (Key Stage 1 and Key Stage 2)
    Drawing vehicles (Key Stage 1)
    Animating pictures (Key Stage 2)

**CHAPTER**

# WORKING MATHEMATICALLY WITH A GRAPHICS PACKAGE

---

The purpose of this chapter is
- to show you some mathematical aspects of graphics packages;
- to encourage you to explore working with graphics yourself.

---

You will get most out of this chapter if you can use a graphics package to try out some of the activities. The facilities offered in graphics packages vary quite a lot, so it would be useful to get hold of the handbook for the one you are using. If you can't find the handbook, it is still worth having a go. You can probably find most things you need just by exploring.

## WHAT IS MATHEMATICAL ABOUT COMPUTER GRAPHICS?

Graphics software varies considerably, from relatively simple packages designed for young children, to very sophisticated ones used by professional artists and designers. Their value for creative work is well recognised, but they also offer possibilities for mathematical activities.

Graphics software generally falls into two categories. **Drawing** packages (such as *Draw* on the Archimedes) generally offer the ability to manipulate objects on the screen, enabling you to produce accurate designs. **Painting** packages (such as *Paintbrush* on the Nimbus) offer a wider range of creative tools and effects, but it is more difficult to alter or adjust your designs once they are on the screen. Colour is obviously an attractive feature, but most children will still find plenty of interest in using graphics on monochrome screens.

Broadly speaking, all graphics software offers the same kinds of basic tools, allowing freehand drawing, or producing straight lines and complete shapes such as circles and rectangles. Additional tools produce different colours and effects, but these are less interesting from a mathematical point of view.

**Explore your graphics software and find out how to use the basic tools.**

## EXPLORING SHAPES

When you use the shape tools, you can click and drag with the mouse until you get the required shape and size. This allows you to explore the effects of changing the proportions of the shapes, and could be used as a focus for discussion with children.

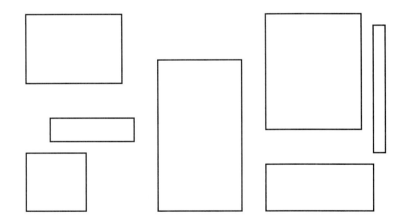

FIGURE 19

Which of the rectangles in figure 19 looks most like a door, or a window, or a book, or a television screen? How could you make a square?

Experimenting with families of circles and curved shapes can be equally interesting. What does each of the shapes in figure 20 look like? How do you have to drag with the mouse to make a circle?

In some packages there may also be a tool for drawing regular polygons, and a menu option to allow you to define how many sides the polygon should have. What happens if you choose a large or very small number of sides? These polygons change size when dragged, but do not change shape, which could also provoke some discussion.

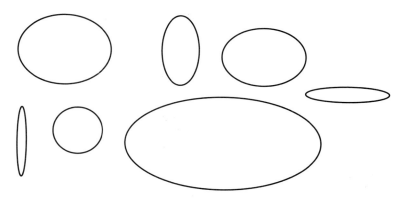

FIGURE 20

**Experiment with making and changing shapes.**

# CHANGING SHAPES

Once you have drawn a particular shape on the screen, most drawing packages will allow you to change it in various ways, although those designed for very young children may not have these facilities. In order to change a shape, you need to **select** it, by clicking on it. A few more sophisticated painting packages offer similar facilities, but objects are selected in a different way: you need to check in your handbook if you are not sure what your software can do.

Depending on the package you are using, you now have a range of possibilities for either changing the shape directly by dragging, or through menu options.

The most basic is to alter the **size** and the **proportions** of the shape. If you cannot do this by dragging, the menus may allow you to **scale** the shape in some way.

Another common feature is the ability to **rotate** the shape, or to **reflect** it about a vertical or horizontal axis. This will sometimes be called a **flip**.

The examples in figure 21 illustrate some of these **transformations**. In order to demonstrate them more clearly, a flag made by combining basic shapes has been used. When working with combinations of shapes you need to make sure they are all selected. You may then be able to **group** them to form a single picture. In the examples, 1 is the original, 2 has been scaled differently in two dimensions, 3 and 4 show reflections and 5 is a rotation.

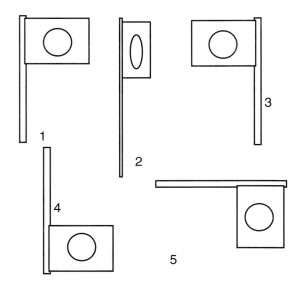

FIGURE 21

In more sophisticated packages, you may be able to transform the shape in other ways (figure 22). Using the words given on the menu in my painting software, example 6 is a **distortion**, 7 is a **shear** and 8 shows the effects of **perspective**. Unfortunately, some of the clarity is lost in these transformations.

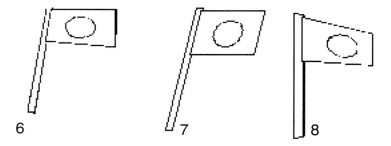

FIGURE 22

# COMBINING SHAPES

The flag that was used in the examples above was drawn by combining two rectangles and a circle: a very simple example of combining shapes to make a picture. Breaking down the image you have in your head into bits that can be made from the drawing tools available can be quite a challenging mathematical activity as well as an artistic one. It requires the same sort of thinking that we might encourage children to develop when they are programming in Logo, breaking down a picture or a problem into separate components which can be dealt with in short procedures.

Children find using computer graphics packages to produce pictures exciting, even if they quickly realise that they can produce some images much more effectively in other media. Some children show remarkable skill and concentration in producing complex drawings. *Michelin Man* and *My Old Teddy* (figure 23) were drawn by Year 5 children, using *ClarisWorks*.

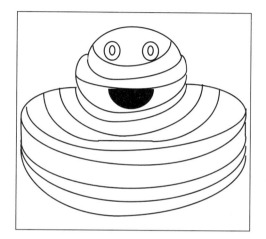 

FIGURE 23

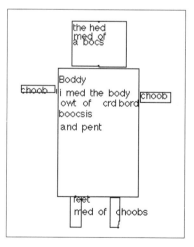

FIGURE 24

As well as combining shapes, most software allows you to combine graphics and text, opening up many further possibilities, including a very effective way of recording and communicating ideas. The report in figure 24 was produced by a six-year-old after a group of children had built a giant out of cardboard boxes and tubes. For this child, integrating words and pictures offered support in the task of writing. Other more confident writers in the class quickly realised that within this particular software (*ClarisWorks*) they could make use of the spelling checker, even when writing on a graphics page!

---

Classroom activities using graphics described in Section B are:

**Chapter 7 Ourselves**
  How we grow (Key Stage 1)

**Chapter 8 Growing and shrinking**
  Scaling pictures (Key Stage 1)
  Creating mazes (Key Stage 1)

**Chapter 9 Exploring patterns**
  Repeating patterns (Key Stage 1)
  Designing wrapping paper (Key Stage 2)

**Chapter 10 Vehicles**
  Drawing vehicles (Key Stage 1 and Key Stage 2)

---

# SECTION B

## USING IT IN CLASSROOM ACTIVITIES

This section is divided into five chapters:

**CHAPTER**

# TAKING IT INTO THE CLASSROOM

In this section of the book, we change emphasis to focus on children using IT in the classroom. Developing your own confidence with using mathematical software is a very important step towards using IT confidently to enrich children's experiences of learning mathematics, but there are many other issues involved which may still pose problems. Throughout this chapter you will occasionally see comments from teachers who have been involved in trying to extend their use of IT in mathematics.

'We don't know the mathematical potential of that machine. We don't have the level of understanding of just what power that machine has. I don't see it as a mathematical tool – yet!'

## DECIDING ON YOUR PRIORITIES

However enthusiastic you feel about using IT for mathematics, making changes in your classroom will take time, and what you are able to do immediately will be limited by a whole range of factors – time, resources, the children's previous experiences, other pressures on the curriculum. It is worth taking some time to think about what you would like to achieve if you *didn't* have these constraints.

'I want computers to become an integrated part of the classroom, just like Unifix or art stuff – not a treat when you have finished your work – an extra resource to support learning. I don't think that would change the work we do, but it would extend it.'

Deciding what you would like to achieve can help you think about what you can do now to move in that direction.

- You might be able to see possibilities for extending one particular area of the mathematics curriculum through using the computer, and focus the resources you have on that.
- You might feel that you can see the potential for one software package, and concentrate on helping the children to get really confident with that, rather than trying to use different pieces of software.

'Using spreadsheets has directly affected what we do in science and mathematics. It has changed the levels the children can go to, for example with interpreting charts and graphs.'

- A topic you already work with might offer an opportunity for mathematical extensions, perhaps through building up a database of children's observations.
- You might decide that it is important to give children a taste of a number of different applications, so that they can start to make their own decisions about which is best for particular tasks.

'It is important for the children to see the computer as a tool that they can use. They are in control of it. Too many people are frightened of computers.'

# DEVELOPING IT SKILLS

One of the issues which regularly concerns teachers is the difficulty of teaching thirty children how to use a complex piece of software, like a spreadsheet. This prospect is particularly threatening for teachers who have only recently mastered using the program themselves. The manuals and handbooks which come with the software are often difficult to use, and not suitable for pupils to use while they are learning.

Two thoughts may make the problem seem less forbidding.

- **Pupils don't need to know everything at once**. Often only a small amount of knowledge is needed to get started, and other techniques can be introduced as they are needed.
- **Teachers don't need to know everything either.** It is perhaps natural to feel that you need to be an 'expert' yourself before you can begin to use software in the classroom, but this really isn't true. To begin with, children will only need a few simple ideas, and if they do get stuck, they will learn more by working through the problem themselves, with your support, than from you solving it for them. If you need to go to the manual, or try something out for yourself, in order to sort out what to do, then the children may learn a valuable lesson in problem-solving skills.

'I'd like to encourage staff to take a computer home and play with it. That might dispel the myth that you have to be a whiz. I don't believe you have to know all the sophisticated things it can do.'

'It was using the computer for something I needed to do that really got me into seeing possibilities. I took it home to do my half-term plans – it took me ages to do some things at first, but I realised I could use it for lots of other things too.'

Research in 'computer-rich' classrooms, where the problem of dealing with many groups of learners at once is particularly acute, suggests that one of the best ways to overcome the problem is to take a radical approach. If you have thirty pupils in your class, then you have thirty potential teachers!

'They learnt a lot more from peer tutoring than they would from just the teacher's input. It was very effective – I can't think how else I could have done it.'

Peer tutoring has proved to be an efficient way of passing on the routine skills involved in using a piece of software. With some preparation about what they need to teach, and how they might approach the task, most children will enjoy taking the role of 'teacher', and be able to pass on their skills in ways which are easy for their friends to grasp. This has the obvious advantage that the teacher's time can be used in other, more productive ways. It can also be a valuable experience for those children who act as tutors; consolidating their own knowledge as well as building self-esteem (figure 25).

FIGURE 25 *Children can tutor each other*

Peer tutoring can be organised in a number of ways. Here are two models which teachers have used successfully.

- **Within a class:** one pair of pupils are introduced to the software by the teacher and given a short task to work on. When they have completed their work, this pair then have the responsibility of introducing the next pair to the software, showing them just enough to get started. The process is repeated, with each pair in the chain taking their turn as tutors, but with the possibility of appealing to *their* tutors for help if they need it.
- **Between classes:** it may sometimes be appropriate to form computer partnerships, similar to the reading partnerships that are fairly common between younger and older children. Children from a class who are already fairly confident with using a particular application are paired with children from a new class. In some cases, groups of four (two tutors and two pupils) may be more effective as it gives both teachers and learners some support. The tutors may need some preparation from their teacher, perhaps making a list of points they need to cover, which incidentally provides an opportunity for 'revision' for those who need it. The initial tutorial may only need a fairly short period, but it can also be productive if the original tutors can continue to act as 'consultants' for some time afterwards, ready to be called in if their tutees have problems.

Less formally, it is easy to encourage children to share their skills within the classroom. Once one group knows how to use the printer, they can show someone else who needs it. The class will quickly get to know who can do what – and of course they will sometimes find out things that you haven't shown them, and perhaps that you don't know yourself. Children often have fewer inhibitions than adults do about exploring technology, and they have very efficient networks for passing this information around, as you will know if you have ever heard children discussing computer games.

Although this might seem quite a frightening prospect at first, take a moment to think about the positive aspects. Remember how you learn to use a new piece of software. The ideal way would be to have someone tell you how to do something just when you need to do it, or someone you could ask for help at any time. If there are thirty or so people in your classroom, it is quite likely that you will get a positive answer to 'Does anyone know how to ...?' And if the children can help each other with practical skills, you can get on with what you are best at – teaching mathematics.

# ORGANISING RESOURCES

One of the difficulties of introducing new software is that it takes time for children to learn how to use it confidently, and if they only use the software occasionally, they may need more time to re-learn the details each time they use it. It is quite clear that, as with many other kinds of learning, children will learn and remember the details of using software more efficiently if they are able to consolidate their learning within a relatively short period. Time spent at the computer concentrated in a short period will lead to much more rapid progress than the same amount of time spread over several weeks. Of course, this may be difficult to arrange when access to computers is limited, and you may have to balance this against wanting to allow equal access to all children .

The IT resources available vary enormously from school to school, but one thing that is likely to be true for all schools is that there will be fewer computers available than you want! Whilst there can be no simple solutions, there may be both short and longer term possibilities for maximising what you do have available.

## *Using what you already have*

If you only have one computer available in your classroom, or worse still, have to share a machine with another class, giving all children enough access to benefit from using a spreadsheet, for example, may seem an impossible task. It need not be. You will need to think carefully about what your priorities are, and think creatively about how you use the resources you have.

Initially, *keep the tasks short*, so that groups can complete a piece of work within a short period, and so keep the momentum going.

*Use the computer to share work.* Children don't need to be using the computer themselves to benefit from its presence in the classroom. Looking at and discussing a graph made by another group may help children to reflect on, or prepare for, their own work on the task. It also gives you an opportunity to reinforce good ideas, and deal with problems efficiently.

Let children *work in small groups* at the computer. It is tempting to make the groups larger, so that more people get a turn quickly, but in practice even three children will often argue about control of the keyboard, and they can easily feel alienated. A shorter time, working amicably with one partner, can be far more productive.

FIGURE 26 *Sharing work with the whole class*

*Children's knowledge accumulates.* It doesn't matter if they only get a little taste of using a spreadsheet this term: next term they can build on that, and perhaps their new teacher can take them further still. What do your class already know that you can build on?

It may also be worth taking a fresh look at how computer resources are distributed within the school. Here are a few possible models for concentrating computer access (assuming a starting point of one machine per class). You can probably think of others that would suit your school situation.

- A time-table in the staff-room saying when particular classes regularly *don't* use their machines (perhaps because of swimming or games) could allow other classes to arrange temporary access to extra machines for short periods.
- Most schools have a variety of computers with different specifications. Some older machines may have quite limited uses, so perhaps it is worth dedicating these to particular applications. For example, older BBC machines will not run more recent software, but can be good for running Logo.
- Two classes could pool their computers, so that each has two machines for half a term, then half a term when they focus on other activities. This could be particularly effective if teachers can work together to plan and evaluate the computer-based work.

- A group of four classes could agree to pool resources on particular days or half-days. For example, once a fortnight each class could have four machines for a whole morning or afternoon, if they give up their machine on three other half-days. This might allow enough time for a whole class to use spreadsheets to support a science activity.

'We have all been surprised at the adaptability the children have shown using the new machines. We wouldn't worry now about using different computers in the classroom; the children have no problems moving from one to another.'

## Looking ahead

When you are looking ahead to purchasing new IT resources, there are now several alternatives to buying desktop machines which are well worth considering. Practically, there is a limit to how many desktop machines a primary school can comfortably hold, whether they are located on trolleys or fixed in classrooms. Small, portable machines offer an exciting alternative. One obvious advantage of portable machines is that they can be taken out of the classroom on school visits, but in the normal school routine, portability can also make a significant difference to the ways in which computers can be used.

Even *within the classroom* portable machines can be used much more naturally than desktop machines. You can have one on your desk alongside books and other resources, or you can take it with you to the book corner, or to a quiet area when you want to concentrate. It's easy to show someone else what you have been doing, but you can also keep it to yourself, which is not easy when you are working on a large screen. If you need help, you can take the machine to someone who can help you.

Because the computer can be used anywhere you want it, *it stops being something special.* It is easier to see the computer as a tool for learning, rather than the computer dominating what is learnt.

Outside the classroom, portable machines are easy to take home. The extra time that this allows for relaxed exploration creates a rapid increase in confidence – and that applies to teachers as much as to children. If the computers go home, the time that they are available for use increases enormously, so a lot more work, and play, gets done.

FIGURE 27 *Portable computers allow you to work where you want to*

(Children taking computers home may sound rather risky, and obviously each school will need to decide what is appropriate and manageable for them. Practically it is not a good idea for children to walk home on their own with valuable equipment, but it is actually safer for machines to be in several different homes over the weekend than all together in school.)

'Coming in to school to pick up the computers helped to get parents involved in the children's work. We found children enjoyed showing the rest of the family what they had learnt.'

Portable computers (often known as Powerbooks or Notebooks) are still relatively expensive, but more specialised portables offer cheaper alternatives. There are really two categories of these. Dedicated **word processors** are just what they sound like: small machines (about A4 size) which can provide children with access to word-processing facilities, but which can't run any other software. Work can be printed out, and a small number of files can be saved on the machine. If you want to save work more permanently, it can be downloaded onto another computer. The price of these machines means that you could buy several for the price of a desktop computer. That could have the combined effect of increasing children's access to word processing, and freeing up other more flexible computers for using mathematical software.

FIGURE 28  *Working with a portable word processor*

Another portable alternative is a **palmtop** or **pocketbook**. These machines run a variety of applications – typically a word processor, spreadsheet, graphing facilities, a calculator, an address book, and often a diary. They are literally pocket-sized, so the screen and keyboard sizes are limited. You might not want to write a novel on one, or design the school newspaper, but they are quite adequate for most of the work primary school children might do with a word processor or a spreadsheet. They can be linked to a printer, or to a desktop machine to download files, though the pocketbook itself will store quite a number of documents. Again the relative prices mean that you might buy half a dozen pocketbooks for the price of a desktop machine.

'If you had six computers in the classroom, you could do the types of things we try to do all the time but actually achieve them.'

## *Looking further afield*

If you really want to get more access to computers for your pupils, one possible source of help might be your local secondary school or FE college. Most secondary schools and colleges have groups of computers located in special IT rooms, which are normally heavily booked. However, at some times of the year, particularly in the summer term when students are taking exams or are on work experience, these rooms may be empty for periods of time. Even if working in an IT 'lab' is not your ideal choice, arranging to borrow a room at a quiet time of year might give you a chance to try a whole class project that you could not otherwise tackle.

# ACTIVITIES FOR THE CLASSROOM

The remaining four chapters are concerned with ways of using computers and calculators to enrich and extend mathematical activities. Each chapter is based around a topic which might form the focus of work in a primary classroom. The mathematical activities that are described arise from the topic, but they are only an indication of what is possible. As you become more confident, you will soon come up with many other ideas which fit into the ways you want to work in your classroom.

# CHAPTER 7

# OURSELVES

The purpose of this chapter is
- to show you some examples of how activities within the topic of *Ourselves* can be developed to enrich children's mathematical thinking.

There is nothing exceptional about the range of activities described in this chapter. They have been deliberately chosen to be familiar, but what is different is the way in which the addition of IT can transform the mathematical experiences of the children.

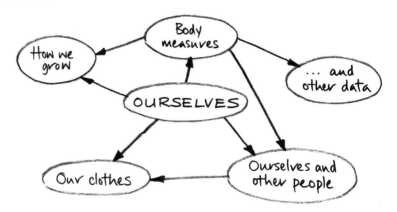

## BODY MEASURES

### *Key Stage 1*

Collecting information about their own body measurements is a familiar activity which generally engages children's interest. Obviously it is an activity which needs to be handled with care if there are children who feel sensitive about their size, but looking at a range of measurements rather than focusing on height or weight can help to diffuse problems.

If children are able to put their measurements onto a computer, either in a spreadsheet or a database, the activity of measuring can be extended in a number of ways.

The need for accuracy while measuring is not always easy for young children to appreciate. The fact that the computer can 'play back' the data that is entered may help them to confront the issues involved.

'Recording their own heights provided a useful way of introducing some six-year-olds to using the computer for drawing graphs. They helped each other to use the height measure in their classroom, and then typed their own name and height into a database that Geoff, their teacher, had already prepared. When Katie's group had finished, Geoff gathered the rest of the class together to see how the graph was made (figure 29). When the graph appeared on the screen, Shari wasn't very happy. "The graph isn't right. Oliver is really the tallest, and Kim is about the same as Tom!"

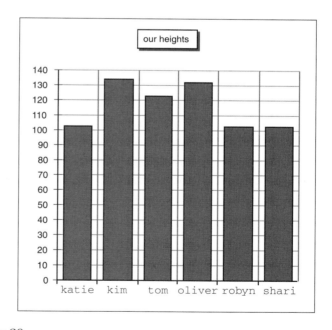

FIGURE 29

Several other voices were raised in protest, so Geoff decided to build on this opportunity. He asked the six children to stand up, and arrange themselves in the order they appeared on the graph. Once the class had agreed about order of the children's real heights, Geoff asked for suggestions about why the graph went wrong. Katie was quick to give her idea: "I think we didn't measure properly, and some people forgot their number before they typed it in".

Geoff was very pleased with the discussion described in this lesson. He was able to talk to the children about ways of measuring more accurately, but he was also keen for the children to be able to look critically at data and graphs, and at what appeared on the computer screen. Some of the children did think that the graph was wrong because the computer had made a mistake, or gone wrong. They would need more experiences of working with the spreadsheet to build their understanding of what the computer could and could not do.

---

**Key mathematical ideas in this activity (Key Stage 1)**

- understanding the language of comparatives
  *Using and Applying Mathematics 3a*
- looking for ways to overcome difficulties
  *Using and Applying Mathematics 2c*
- collecting, recording and interpreting data *Number 5b*
- using standard units of length *Shape, Space and Measures 4a*
- using simple measuring instruments *Shape, Space and Measures 4b*

---

## Key Stage 2

Measuring and recording data about themselves is still an appropriate and interesting activity for older children, where the range of measures and the level of accuracy required may be increased. They may need to use fractions of units, particularly for looking at shorter lengths, such as the lengths of hands and feet. The fact that the computer will not accept fractions may provide a good opportunity to introduce or reinforce decimal equivalents of common fractions such as halves and quarters.

Collecting measurements, or indeed any other data, for their own sake is of rather limited interest, but once you have the data on the computer it can be used for a whole range of activities and investigations. Some of these extend into the other sections of this chapter.

If you are going to collect a large amount of data, such as taking several different body measurements from the whole class, how you set up the database or spreadsheet becomes a significant issue. The way in which the data is set out and entered can affect how it can be used. One approach would be to set up the framework for the children, as Geoff had done in the previous example, so that children have a good model to follow. Another approach is to let the children experiment with their own methods, and then discuss their advantages and disadvantages. In most cases, layouts can easily be rearranged, so the children's initial efforts will not be wasted.

'Some eight- and nine-year-olds had begun collecting their body measurements, working in small groups. In the first session, most had recorded their work on paper, but two groups had used a spreadsheet to store their data. Their teacher Celia had let each group decide how they would lay out the spreadsheet, but she realised that if they wanted to draw graphs later on, they would need some help to choose an appropriate layout.

At the beginning of the next lesson, Celia gathered the class on the carpet around the computer, and asked the two groups to share the spreadsheets they had started. Tom's group had set their work out like this (figure 30).

|    | A     | B           | C     |
|----|-------|-------------|-------|
| 1  | Tom   | foot length | 17cm  |
| 2  | Lee   | foot length | 18cm  |
| 3  | Julie | foot length | 17cm  |
| 4  | Tom   | waist       | 65cm  |
| 5  | Lee   | waist       |       |
| 6  | Julie | waist       |       |
| 7  | Tom   | head        |       |
| 8  | Lee   | head        |       |
| 9  | Julie | head        |       |
| 10 |       |             |       |

FIGURE 30

Although the information was clear, the teacher explained tactfully that it might not be the best layout for everything they wanted to do.

|   | A       | B      | C     | D           | E   |
|---|---------|--------|-------|-------------|-----|
| 1 |         | height | waist | foot length | arm |
| 2 | Laura   | 125 cm | 73 cm |             |     |
| 3 | Ambreen | 127 cm |       |             |     |
| 4 | Mandy   | 133 cm |       |             |     |
| 5 | Liam    | 121 cm |       |             |     |
| 6 |         |        |       |             |     |
| 7 |         |        |       |             |     |

FIGURE 31

Fortunately, Laura's group had used a different method, which seemed more efficient (figure 31).

This layout could be easily extended and used for producing graphs. However, the children also needed to know that the spreadsheet could not understand entries like 125 cm. Celia explained that the computer was not as clever as them, and needed to know clearly which were numbers and which were words. She helped Laura to alter her spreadsheet to avoid the problem, and they were then able to graph their heights easily (figure 32).'

|   | A | B | C | D | E |
|---|---|---|---|---|---|
| 1 |   | height in cms | waist | foot length | arm |
| 2 | Laura | 125 |   |   |   |
| 3 | Ambreen | 127 |   |   |   |
| 4 | Mandy | 133 |   |   |   |
| 5 | Liam | 121 |   |   |   |
| 6 |   |   |   |   |   |
| 7 |   |   |   |   |   |

FIGURE 32

Although Laura's method was a good one, it will still present some problems when the group want to make other graphs, because on many spreadsheets you can only graph data from columns that are next to each other. So, in order to make a graph of waist measures, they would need to create a new column next to column C and then copy the list of names in column A into it (figure 33). (Notice that when you create a new column, the column labels adjust themselves.) This may sound complicated, but it actually only involves a few key presses, and children will learn the sequence very quickly.

|   | A | B | C | D | E |
|---|---|---|---|---|---|
| 1 |   | height in cms |   | waist | foot length |
| 2 | Laura | 125 | Laura |   |   |
| 3 | Ambreen | 127 | Ambreen |   |   |
| 4 | Mandy | 133 | Mandy |   |   |
| 5 | Liam | 121 | Liam |   |   |
| 6 |   |   |   |   |   |
| 7 |   |   |   |   |   |

FIGURE 33

Once the collection of data is complete, the children can begin to look at the kinds of information they can find from it, and the questions they can answer. There are two main techniques which they might use: drawing graphs and sorting the data.

There are some obvious straightforward questions, such as

- Who is the tallest?
- Who has the smallest feet?
- Who has the longest arms?

These may be useful for helping the children to become familiar with how to manipulate the data, although they are perhaps of limited interest. Working on these questions may also encourage children to look critically at the accuracy of their data.

'Ben and Romy decided to use their turn at the computer to look at the size of ears amongst their class. They began by drawing a bar graph, but were a bit surprised by what they saw (figure 34). At first they just said that Phillipa had the biggest ears, but then when they showed the graph to some other children they realised that something might be wrong. After going back to the data, they got out a ruler and measured out the length that had been recorded for Phillipa's ears. It was clearly not a reasonable length for any human ears! They found Phillipa and re-measured her ears.'

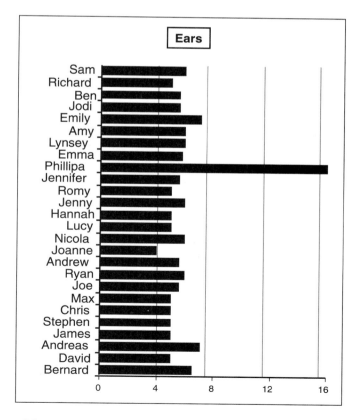

FIGURE 34

Experiences like this one are valuable not just for making children realise the importance of accuracy in measuring and entering data, but also for sharpening their skills in interpreting graphs. At first they looked only at the shape of the graph, without taking notice of the scales on the axes. It also made a starting point for the teacher to talk about the idea of a reasonable range within the data, and to encourage them to make estimates.

As children explore graphing on the spreadsheet, they will inevitably want to try out the different kinds of graph on offer. Sometimes they may choose graphs which are not appropriate either for the data they have, or for the question they want to explore. Children are often attracted by more unusual graphs, such as pie charts, particularly if the software allows them to create interesting graphic effects. The examples in figure 35 were produced from data collected about body measurements.

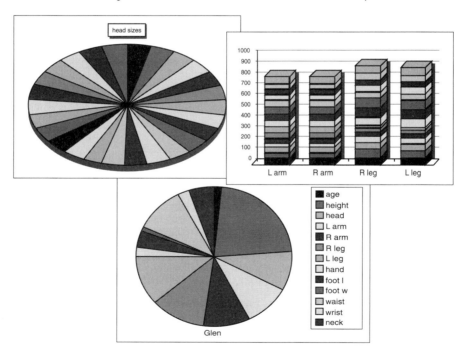

FIGURE 35

The three-dimensional pie chart has been drawn from data about the head sizes of a large group of children. Even with a key, it would be impossible to use it to compare the sizes, and the whole 'pie' represents the total of all the measurements, which does not make much sense.

The stacked bar chart has been drawn from data about the lengths of children's arms and legs. Each child has a slice in each bar, but again it is impossible to interpret the information the graph contains.

The final pie chart was made from all the data Glen had collected about himself, including his age. Different units and measures have been combined, making the graph completely nonsensical.

It is easy to see these nonsense graphs as 'mistakes' or 'problems', but they can be an important stage in children's understanding of graphing. When children choose these graphs, they are focusing on their appearance rather than what they can be used for. The experience which some children have of making graphs without a computer is to collect some data, draw the graph and then display it: it isn't surprising that they see graphs as decorative rather than useful.

By looking more carefully at the graphs they make on the computer, including the nonsense graphs, we can help children to appreciate the importance of being able to interpret the information they contain. Try pointing to a particular part of the graph and asking children what it shows, or reading information from the graph yourself which clearly does not make sense. Obviously confronting children with these problems needs to be done tactfully, but the fact that graphs can be changed so easily on the computer makes the activity less threatening than it might otherwise be.

This is also a good example of the limitations of the computer. It is completely uncritical, and will process nonsense as efficiently as useful information. Although the computer appears to eliminate the need for the skills of producing graphs, it requires the user to exercise higher level skills in selecting and interpreting information.

---

### Key mathematical ideas in this activity  (Key Stage 2)

- devising and refining their own ways of recording *Using and Applying Mathematics 1c*
- checking results to see if they are reasonable *Using and Applying Mathematics 2d*
- presenting information and results clearly *Using and Applying Mathematics 3c*
- using appropriate measuring instruments, and interpreting numbers *Shape, Space and Measures 4b*
- collecting and representing data appropriately using graphs *Handling Data 2b*
- drawing conclusions from graphs and recognising why some may be misleading *Handling Data 2d*

## *More interesting questions*

Children who are reasonably confident with working with the spreadsheet can look at some more interesting and challenging questions, depending of course on what data you have collected.

- Do the tallest people have the largest feet?
- Could you predict someone's height from the length of their arms?
- David's right foot is longer than his left foot: is that true for other people?
- Do girls have bigger hands than boys?

To investigate questions like these, children will need to use a range of approaches. Sorting data in various ways will be useful, and in some cases different kinds of graphs may be needed. Graphing the sizes of left and right feet as shown in figure 36 might make it easier to extract the information.

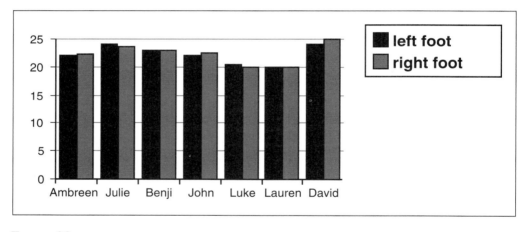

FIGURE 36

Sometimes children will need to decide exactly what they want to know before they can choose the most appropriate graph.

'Joanne's group wanted to investigate the suggestion that tall people have big feet. Before they started they agreed that they thought this would be true. They used the computer to sort the data according to height, and drew a bar graph. Then they sorted the data again, this time using foot length, and drew another bar graph. When they looked at their two graphs (figure 37), they still weren't sure what they had found out.

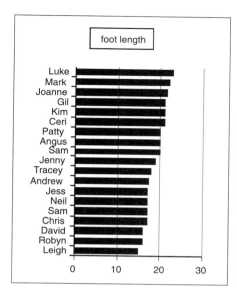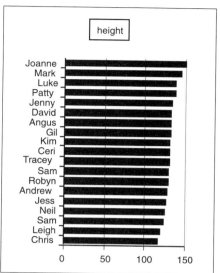

FIGURE 37

Joanne thought that their prediction was wrong: she was the tallest person, but she didn't have the biggest feet. David noticed that Joanne, Mark and Luke were the top three people in both lists, so he thought that their prediction was right. Some of the others felt that if the tallest people had the biggest feet, the order would have to be just the same on both graphs.'

For investigating this question, it would be more appropriate to use a different kind of graph altogether. A scattergraph allows you to look at how two variables are related generally, without focusing on individual cases. The children's confusion offered a good opportunity to introduce this new kind of graph (figure 38).

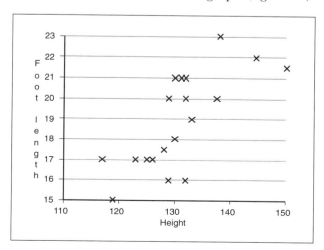

FIGURE 38

Looking at the pattern of crosses in different regions of the graph, it is fairly clear that most of the crosses are in a line from the bottom left to the top right: in other words, as height increases, foot length increases. Children may begin by looking at particular crosses, perhaps trying to identify themselves. Describing the properties of a particular cross – say, pointing at the one on the horizontal axis which shows someone who is quite short and has small feet – can offer a way into talking more generally about the pattern.

---

**Key mathematical ideas in this activity (Key Stage 2)**

- asking questions and following alternative suggestions to support reasoning *Using and Applying Mathematics 1d*
- presenting information and results clearly *Using and Applying Mathematics 3c*
- explaining their reasoning *Using and Applying Mathematics 4d*
- using appropriate measuring instruments, and interpreting numbers *Shape, Space and Measures 4b*
- collecting information through undertaking purposeful enquiries *Handling Data 1b*
- interpreting a wider range of graphs *Handling Data 2b*
- drawing conclusions from graphs and recognising why some may be misleading *Handling Data 2d*

---

## ... AND OTHER DATA

### *Key Stages 1 and 2*

There are other kinds of data which children might collect about themselves as well as body measures. They might also record other physical characteristics, such as hair and eye colour, numbers of brothers and sisters, or preferences in food, colours or sports. For this it might be better to use a database rather than a spreadsheet, as this is better suited for entering and handling data in words, although if you only have a spreadsheet you could carry out some of the same activities.

It is important to spend time discussing which data to collect, and how to record it so that it can be accessed easily. It is time consuming to set up a lot of records, so it is well worth having a 'test run' at an early stage to sort out any problems. For example, when entering eye colours, children might use a number of different descriptions for similar colours: green, brown, greeny brown, brown and green, brown/green, hazel. There are a number of ways of resolving this. One approach would be to draw up a list of alternatives from which to choose. In some databases this can be actually put into the software, so that the user only has to select the choice they want. With less sophisticated software, you may need to agree a list for reference. Other approaches would be to use a code, such as a single letter or a number for each choice, or to ask a series of yes/no questions.

In deciding which is best for you, you will need to consider what you will want to do with the data. If you want to be able to pick out all the people with each eye colour separately, it would be no good to enter brown/green for hazel eyes, as this person would then be included in both the brown and the green group.

This wider collection of data offers scope for investigating a different range of questions.

- Are there any patterns in the colours of children's hair and eyes?
- Do girls choose the same favourite lessons as boys?
- Which month are the tallest people born in?

It is also possible to look at which characteristics or preferences are most common. Using a database, particularly one that has been produced for educational use, it is often possible to make graphs which show categories of data. For example, the graph in figure 39 could be made to show the distribution of eye colours.

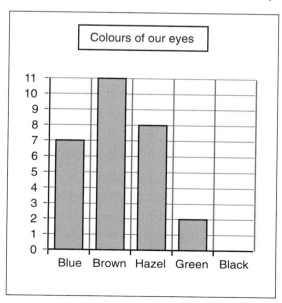

FIGURE 39

It would not be possible to draw this graph from the same data recorded on a spreadsheet, which could only graph numerical data.

---

**Key mathematical ideas in this activity  (Key Stage 1)**

- sorting and classifying *Number 5a*
- collecting, recording and interpreting data, using a range of graphs *Number 5b*

**(Key Stage 2)**

- using diagrams and graphs *Using and Applying Mathematics 3b*
- presenting information clearly *Using and Applying Mathematics 3c*
- collecting and representing discrete data *Handling Data 2b*
- interpreting a wider range of graphs *Handling Data 2b*
- drawing conclusions from graphs and recognising why some may be misleading *Handling Data 2d*

---

# HOW WE GROW

## *Key Stage 1*

Children are always fascinated by their own life histories, and a good way to extend and develop work on body measures is to look at how those measurements have changed since they were babies. This will involve the children in some research at home, finding information about themselves when they were born, or at different ages. Parents may be able to find baby records, or perhaps a height chart they have been keeping at home. Of course, if the records are marked up the door frame it may be tricky to bring them in to school! (There may be an issue over the use of metric and imperial measures: that might appear to be a problem you need to smooth out, or an opportunity to talk about the different systems.)

Discussing their findings will be made easier if children are able to put their data onto a spreadsheet and produce a graph to look at alongside the numerical information (figure 40).

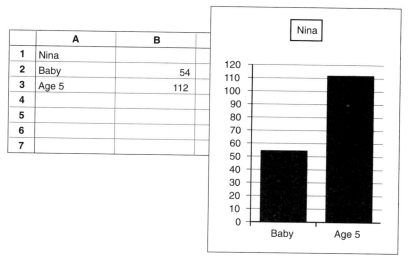

FIGURE 40

The visual image makes it easier to consider questions like '*Am I twice as tall now as I was when I was born?*' If other records are available, you could go on to compare those as well: 'I'm about twice as tall – am I twice as heavy?'

Children may also enjoy comparing their heights to those of adults and older siblings. Collecting some data about the whole family could offer opportunities for developing the vocabulary of comparisons, and perhaps for making predictions about their future growth. Using the visual feedback from graphs can support children's understanding of the relatively large numbers involved.

After discussions about the relative sizes of people of different ages, trying to make drawings which reflect these proportions can help to consolidate children's ideas. It is worth considering different media for this activity. Producing the picture with pencil or paints may be artistically satisfying, but pictures made by cutting out shapes may encourage more comparisons. Similarly, using computer graphics offers a different experience again, as sizes can be adjusted and re-adjusted many times without spoiling the finished result.

Children who have some experience with Logo may be able to make more direct links between numbers and the sizes of pictures produced.

'Margaret's class had already used Logo for drawing, but she wanted to extend their thinking about relative sizes by creating Logo families. Because of the limited time available, she decided to provide them with a ready-made procedure, in which they could change the sizes (figure 41).

```
to person :hsize :bod :arm :leg      to arms :arm
pu bk 50 pd                          bk :bod/3
legs :leg                            lt 60 fd :arm bk :arm
body :bod                            rt 120 fd :arm bk :arm
arms :arm                            lt 60 fd :bod/3
head :hsize                          end
end

                                     to head :hsize
to legs :leg                         lt 90
rt 20 fd :leg                        repeat 36 [fd :hsize rt 10]
rt 140 fd :leg bk :leg               rt 90
lt 160                               end
end

to body :bod
fd :bod
end
```

FIGURE 41

The procedure was built from four subprocedures which drew the
legs, body, arms and head, and needed four input numbers to control
the sizes of these. Margaret showed a small group of children that they
could draw a person using person 3 50 40 60, and then encouraged
them to explore what happened if they used different numbers.

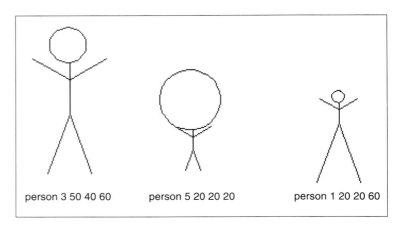

person 3 50 40 60        person 5 20 20 20        person 1 20 20 60

FIGURE 42

To begin with, the children struggled to get a sense of how the four
numbers affected the drawing, and they produced some very strange
effects (figure 42). Margaret intervened to suggest that they kept a
written record of the numbers they tried, and what happened. This
helped them to feel more in control, and they gradually began to
make predictions about what they thought would happen, and
managed to make people of different sizes who 'looked right'.

> **Key mathematical ideas in this activity  (Key Stage 1)**
>
> * understanding the language of number and comparatives
>   *Using and Applying Mathematics 3a*
> * comparing objects using appropriate language *Shape, Space and Measures 4a*

## Key Stage 2

If older children are able to collect information about their own growth, the most appropriate way to display it is as a line graph. Drawing these graphs by hand involves a whole range of skills, which may seem daunting, but using a spreadsheet makes it possible to produce the graph quickly, and then discuss and analyse it.

'Pinder made this graph with help from Moira, his teacher (figure 43). He had found out his height at various ages from birth to age three. He showed it to the rest of the class.

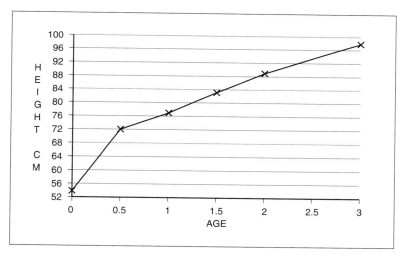

FIGURE 43

Immediately Emily said: "It says two-and-a-half there (i.e. on the axis) but that wasn't in the spreadsheet". Moira asked if they could work out how tall Pinder was when he was two-and-a-half. Several ideas were offered.

Debby: "Would it be half way along that part of the line?"

Jason: "You could look at the numbers and work out half way between them."

A number of other children moved their fingers in the air, apparently trying to read off the height on the vertical axis, although they found it difficult to articulate what it was they wanted to do. The discussion which followed indicated that the children were able to make sense of the information contained in the graph, even though they had not been taught about scales and axes.'

From this starting point, children could go on to look at the growth charts that are used by health visitors and doctors, and try to predict their own adult heights.

---

**Key mathematical ideas in this activity  (Key Stage 2)**

- trying different mathematical approaches *Using and Applying Mathematics  2b*
- interpreting a wider range of graphs *Handling Data 2b*
- drawing conclusions from statistics and graphs *Handling Data 2d*

---

# OURSELVES AND OTHER PEOPLE

## *Key Stage 2*

A natural extension of the activity of collecting body measures is to move from looking at ourselves as individuals to ourselves as a group. There is a need for some sensitivity here, as in other activities, if there are children who feel some anxiety about their size, but looking at the group as a whole can also be a way of introducing anonymity.

A useful tool for considering a group of people is the *average*. There are actually three measures of average which are used in mathematics, but to begin with let's work with the most common; the *mean*. This is the average which is calculated by totalling the values involved and then dividing by the number of items considered. (The mean average of 27, 35, 42 and 50 is $154 \div 4 = 38.5$)

Working with a computer can allow children to work with the idea of average, and get a sense of what it is and how it can be useful, before they need to struggle with the calculations. In the example given above the calculation is fairly straightforward, but when dealing with real, messy data the calculations can be much harder and more time consuming.

The computer can support children's understanding in three ways. Graphs can be used to offer a visual image of the mean which may be a powerful starting point. Spreadsheets and databases generally have a built in function to calculate the mean automatically. Finally, the possibility of handling large quantities of data easily means that children can tackle activities which show ways in which the mean average can be used to solve realistic problems.

Children's ideas about the meaning of 'average', derived from its common usage, may well be to do with being 'in the middle'. Working from the visual image of a graph can be helpful in developing this idea with more precision. Starting with a bar graph of children's heights, for example, and moving a horizontal line up and down, can be used to estimate the average height. The idea is to find a point where the portions of the taller bars above the line would fill the gaps between the shorter bars and the line. In an integrated software package such as *ClarisWorks* or *Microsoft Works*, it may be possible to put a line from the graphics tools onto the graph, and move it directly on the screen. Other possibilities would be to use a ruler, a length of string or a line drawn on an acetate sheet in front of the screen, or to print the graph and add lines on paper.

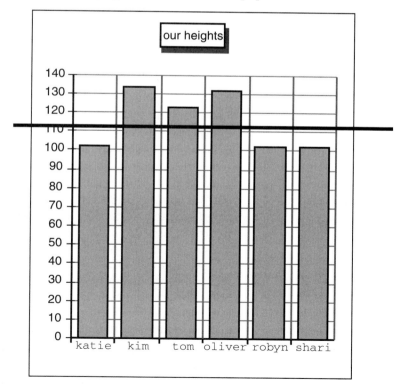

FIGURE 44

The value of this activity, particularly as a focus for group discussion, is that it gives a sense of the way in which the mean is found by balancing extremes, without having to be concerned with precise values. Sorting the data before you draw the graph will give a different image, which you may find easier to work with, but it may also lead to some confusion with the other measures of average discussed later.

Children could go on to compare their visual estimates with the precise value calculated using the average function on the spreadsheet or database. (Although this is often named just as the average, it always refers to the mean average.)

'After a discussion around the computer in which they had used the spreadsheet function to find the average height of the class, Matthew, Alex, Jose and Asif wanted to know which children were the average height. They went back to the original data they had collected, but were very puzzled to find that no one exactly matched the average height the computer had given. This seemed to undermine the ideas they had formed about what the average meant.

Dave, their teacher, took them back to looking at a graph, this time working with just the data about the four of them. They moved a line on the graph, and did agree that the place that it 'balanced' was not quite on the top of anybody's bar. When Dave came back to talk to them again, they wanted to know how the computer worked out the average. He got them to imagine sticking all the bars of the graph together into one long strip, and then cutting it into four equal pieces.'

The mean average is a very powerful tool for addressing a whole range of questions which could have arisen from activities in the two previous sections. The question *Do girls have bigger hands than boys?* could be tackled by looking at individuals, but might be answered better by looking at girls and boys as two groups; taking the average hand sizes for boys and for girls.

But of course children may also realise that this is only a limited solution, since they are only looking at girls and boys from one age group. If the average hand size for girls is bigger than for boys amongst the nine-year-olds, is it also true for the youngest and the oldest children in the school? The computer can handle large quantities of data, and enable children to undertake investigations of this kind. Collecting the data will require co-operation from other classes, but planning how it can be collected most efficiently will be a valuable activity in itself, focusing children's attention on a number of mathematical issues. Entering the data into the computer should not prove too time consuming, particularly as there is no need to collect the names of individual children. A parent or other adult helper with some typing skills may be useful to speed things up.

Some investigations may be particularly interesting across different age groups, as some of the proportions of our bodies change as we grow, for example, the size of our heads relative to our height or the length of our arms changes throughout childhood. In fact in some developing countries where children's dates of birth are not accurately recorded, the ability to touch your left ear by putting your right arm over your head (or vice versa) is used as a way of judging that children are old enough to start school.

## Other measures of average

There are two other measures of average which are used by mathematicians: the median and the mode. These are both found by manipulating the information you have, rather than by a calculation, and a computer can be used to make this manipulation easier. It is less easy to find situations in which young children might find these two measures useful, but they are included here for completeness.

The *mode* is used to show the most commonly occurring value in a set of data. It is appropriate for considering discrete data, such as shoe size, rather than continuous data such as height or weight. The mode is found simply by counting how often each value occurs, and finding the most common (figure 45). Sorting the data on a spreadsheet makes it easier to count efficiently. If the data is stored in a database, it may be possible to draw a frequency graph (as described in the earlier section '... and other data') which will make it easy to read off the mode.

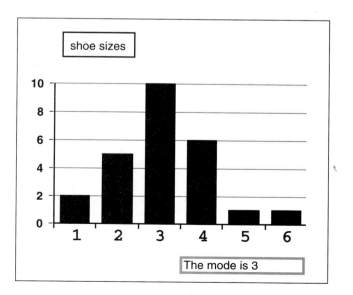

FIGURE 45

The *median* is the middle value of a set of data, and it is found by putting the values in order, and then selecting the middle one (figure 46). This can be done very easily with data that is entered in a spreadsheet which can then be sorted into order.

These values could, of course, also be graphed, or the activity could be personalised by getting the children themselves to stand in a row in order of height.

In examining and discussing tables of data and graphs to find the median or the mode, children may also begin to look at the *distribution* and the *range* of the data – ideas which will be important for later studies in statistics.

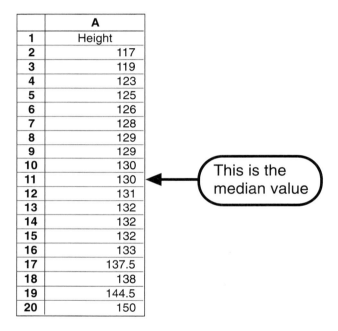

| | A |
|---|---|
| **1** | Height |
| **2** | 117 |
| **3** | 119 |
| **4** | 123 |
| **5** | 125 |
| **6** | 126 |
| **7** | 128 |
| **8** | 129 |
| **9** | 129 |
| **10** | 130 |
| **11** | 130 |
| **12** | 131 |
| **13** | 132 |
| **14** | 132 |
| **15** | 132 |
| **16** | 133 |
| **17** | 137.5 |
| **18** | 138 |
| **19** | 144.5 |
| **20** | 150 |

This is the median value

FIGURE 45

---

**Key mathematical ideas in this activity  (Key Stage 2)**

- searching for patterns in results *Using and Applying Mathematics 4b*
- understanding and using measures of average and range *Handling Data 2c*
- drawing conclusions from statistics and graphs *Handling Data 2d*

# OUR CLOTHES

## *Key Stage 2*

Clothing can be a rich topic in itself, and children could carry out a range of activities in science and technology, such as testing the qualities of various fabrics, or exploring methods of constructing garments, where the computer would be a useful tool for storing and handling the data they collect. Mathematical ideas will inevitably be important in these activities.

For example, to test how effective different fabrics are in keeping us warm, you could set up an experiment using each fabric to insulate a beaker of hot water, and take the temperature at regular intervals. Data from several different experiments could be compared by producing line graphs of the results. (It would also be possible to use a temperature sensor with software which allows the data to be recorded directly onto the computer. This technique is known as data logging.)

---

**Key mathematical ideas in this activity  (Key Stage 2)**

- using appropriate measuring instruments with increasing accuracy *Shape, Space and Measures 4b*
- using a wider range of graphs *Handling Data 2b*
- drawing conclusions from statistics and graphs *Handling Data 2d*

---

A development of the activities with body measures would be to look at how clothes are designed to fit people of different sizes. Children may be aware of many of their own clothes being sized according to age and/or height. This raises a number of questions that they might investigate.

- How do the manufacturers decide how tall a ten-year-old is?
- Do they use the same sizes for boys and girls?
- How well do the ages on their clothes match their real ages?
- If the sizing is based on height, how do they decide what size to make the waist?
- If some clothes, like trousers, are sold by the waist size, how do they decide how long to make them?
- How are clothes for adults sized?

Investigating these questions will provide opportunities for using many of the techniques already described in this chapter. Linking sizes to ages of children is a real world example where finding the average is useful. (A question you might want to think about, but not necessarily share with the children, is whether manufacturers actually use the mean or the mode. Would these give the same value for the children in your class?)

In order to think about how trouser lengths are linked to waist sizes, for example, a scattergraph of leg length against waist size drawn from data stored on a spreadsheet or database would give a clear picture. Children might also need the idea of the *line of best fit*, that is a line drawn through the densest mass of crosses on the graph, which gives an average conversion factor. The graph in figure 47 shows an attempt at putting a line of best fit through data about leg and waist lengths collected by a class of eight- and nine-year-olds. The data does not give a very clear picture as the crosses are quite scattered. This may be the result of rather inaccurate measurements, or it may show that there is not a clear correlation between these two factors for this age group. However, if we are happy to accept this line as a rough estimate, we could use it to read off average values as shown in the table below.

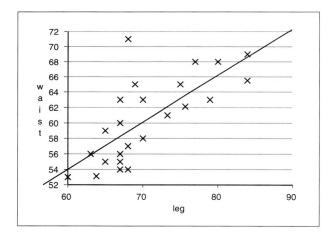

| leg | waist |
|-----|-------|
| 60 cm | 54 cm |
| 70 cm | 60 cm |
| 80 cm | 66 cm |
| 90 cm | 72 cm |

FIGURE 47

(If you are thinking that these values look unrealistic, you need to know that the children measured their outside leg length, rather than the inside leg measurement we normally use!)

'Barry organised a visit to the local department store for his class of eight- and nine-year-olds. They were shown around the clothing departments, and looked at how adults' clothes were sized. They realised that some clothes were sized in two ways: men's trousers by waist and leg length, women's coats by size and length.

In the shoe department, they were shown how the stock was stored, so that the sales assistants could find everything easily. The manager explained how they only stocked certain sizes, but could order very large or very small sizes from the warehouse. He also explained how the computer was used to keep track of the stock. They could check on the screen whether they had a particular pair of shoes in stock, without having to search through the shelves.

After the visit, Barry was able to build on this experience to help the children get a sense of the mode as a measure of average (though he didn't use this term with the children). They looked back at their own body measures, and discussed what size shoes a shop ought to stock for children of their age.

Barry also gave them some other questions to discuss.

- At the local bowling rink you have to hire special shoes; how could the manager decide how many pairs of each size shoes to stock?
- Men's trousers seem to be sold in about six different waist sizes, and three different lengths. How many different sizes do the manufacturers have to make? Do you think they make the same number of pairs in each size?

At this stage, the children were really only able to discuss these questions in general terms. They would have needed access to a lot more data in order to answer them properly. However, Barry felt that some of the children were beginning to get a sense of the mathematical ideas involved, even though others would need more experiences later to see their significance.'

---

### Key mathematical ideas in this activity  (Key Stage 2)

- selecting and using the appropriate mathematics *Using and Applying Mathematics 2a*
- identifying the information needed to carry out a task *Using and Applying Mathematics 2b*
- understanding and investigating general statements *Using and Applying Mathematics 4a*
- making general statements of their own *Using and Applying Mathematics 4c*
- using a wider range of graphs *Handling Data 2b*
- understanding and using meausres of average *Handling data 2c*
- drawing conclusions from statistics and graphs *Handling Data 2d*

# CHAPTER 8

# GROWING AND SHRINKING

The purpose of this chapter is
- to show you some examples of how activities within the topic of *Growing and shrinking* can be developed to enrich children's mathematical thinking.

There is nothing exceptional about the range of activities described in this chapter. They have been deliberately chosen to be familiar, but what *is* different is the way in which the addition of IT can transform the mathematical experiences of the children.

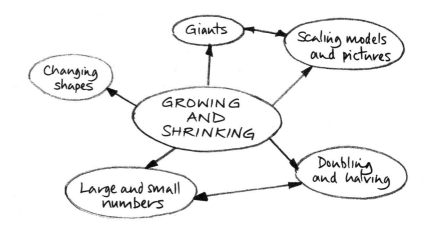

## GIANTS

### *Key Stage 1*

Activities around the idea of giants are generally exciting and stimulating for children, and lead to all sorts of imaginative and creative initiatives. Mathematically they offer rich opportunities for working on comparisons of size, and basic ideas of scaling and proportion. The first description of an activity with giants comes from the same class as the example recording how the giant was built near the end of Chapter 5.

'Hazel's group built a model giant from cardboard boxes and other junk materials. They had been measuring their own heights, and so they decided to measure their giant. They added his measurement to the spreadsheet, and produced this graph (figure 48).

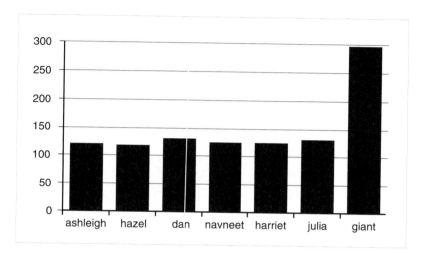

FIGURE 48

They were impressed by how much taller than them the giant looked on the graph. They were able to make this comparison more easily from the graph, than from standing beside their model. For some reason it seemed easier to see the whole picture.'

The children's spontaneous interest in comparing their heights with the giant's could be developed and extended by thinking about objects the giant might use (as in *Jim and the Beanstalk*, Raymond Briggs, 1973). In this case, the giant was about twice the height of the children. Using this information, the children could try to make models of familiar objects – a pencil, a plate, shoes – which would be the right size for the giant. This would involve measuring which, depending on the units used, might produce large or awkward numbers which the children could not double easily. This need not be a barrier if calculators are to hand, and working out how to use the calculator to double their measurements may be an interesting challenge for some children (see 'Doubling and halving' later in this chapter).

> **Key mathematical ideas in this activity  (Key Stage 1)**
>
> - understanding the language of comparatives *Using and Applying Mathematics 3a*
> - discussing their work, responding to and asking mathematical questions *Using and Applying Mathematics 3c*
> - recognising simple patterns and relationships, and making predictions about them *Using and Applying Mathematics  4a*
> - comparing objects, using standard units of length *Shape, Space and Measures 4a*
> - using simple measuring instruments *Shape, Space and Measures 4b*

## Key Stage 2

Older children can still find the idea of giants a fascinating one, and will be able to take the ideas of relative size further.

'To set the scene for a giant investigation, Phyllis made a photocopy of her hand, and then enlarged it. She told the class a story about meeting a (female) giant while she was on holiday, and asked if they could work out, from the copy of her hand, how tall she was. After some discussion, they realised that they needed to know about the sizes of their own hands and their heights. They began collecting measurements, and Phyllis helped them to record the information on a spreadsheet. They added Phyllis' measurements as well.

Once they had collected the data, Phyllis showed them how they could display it on a scattergraph. Most of the children had never seen this kind of graph before, so they needed to spend some time discussing it. They could identify the teacher's point on the graph easily, but although some children were keen to find their own marks, this proved difficult to do.

Phyllis asked them to think about what marks in different areas of the graph would mean: a mark near the top left corner would be a tall person with very small hands, and so on. They finally agreed that the graph showed that generally taller people had bigger hands, which was what most of them had expected.

Phyllis then asked where the giant's mark would come on the graph. Nico realised that the graph wasn't big enough to put the giant's mark on, because the horizontal axis only went up to 20, and the giant's hand was 23 cm. Phyllis demonstrated how to change the axes, to make the graph bigger, and showed them how to add a line of best fit to the graph, to help them estimate where the giant's mark should go (figure 49). They read off the giant's height as about 230 cm.

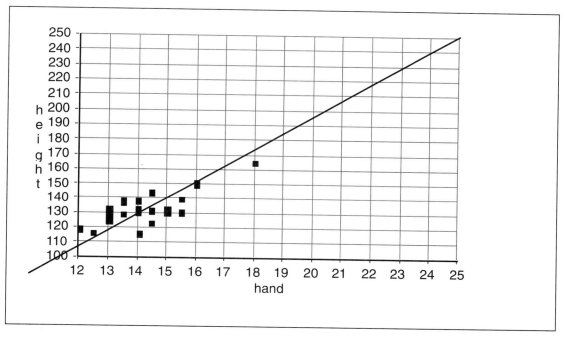

FIGURE 49

Nico and Rachel fixed a label on the wall to show how tall the giant was. Later in the week, the class began making some belongings for the giant. They used hand sizes as an informal unit of measure. Jesse and Michael measured the size of one of their jumpers using their own hand lengths, and then used a strip of card the same length as the giant's hand to measure out a giant jumper.'

In retrospect, Phyllis felt she would make some changes if she did this activity again. Putting a line of best fit on the graph was not easy, as the data was very scattered, but also bunched in a small range. Next time she would to pay more attention to accurate measurement, and also collect a wider range of data from adults in the school.

The other aspect she wants to change is the actual size of the giant's hand. If this was made to be a size which was in a simple ratio to the children's own hands, some of the children would have been able to tackle the second part of the activity through calculations using a scale factor, rather than using informal units.

**Key mathematical ideas in this activity  (Key Stage 2)**

- selecting and using appropriate mathematics *Using and Applying Mathematics 2a*
- making general statements based on evidence they have produced *Using and Applying Mathematics 4a*
- using appropriate measuring instruments *Shape, Space and Measures 4a*
- collecting and representing data and interpreting a wider range of graphs *Handling Data 2b*

**(Key Stages 3 and 4)**

- developing an understanding of scale and enlarging shapes *Shape, Space and Measures 3d*

# SCALING MODELS AND PICTURES

## *Key Stage 1*

Some ideas for simple scaling activities have already been mentioned under the heading of 'Giants'. Similar possibilities obviously exist for scaling down models, for example creating dolls' houses or scenes for other imaginative play. Much of this modelling may be done by eye, without any reference to measurement, but the opportunities are there for introducing appropriate language and more precision as the children are ready for it. Using a calculator for, say, halving a measurement will mean talking specifically about halving as dividing by two.

The idea of scaling may also arise when children are working with pictures created on the computer.

'Leroy wanted to make a picture of a giant's family. He created a picture using the graphics program, selected the picture and then stretched it (figure 50). He was rather surprised by the results, and had to begin to think about proportions in two dimensions.'

Working with Logo also offers opportunities for discussion about changing the size of a picture. Children will need to think about the distances they use for making different versions of the same picture, such as chairs for the three bears. Six- and seven-year-olds who have had experience of drawing and writing procedures in Logo may be able to tackle the idea of including a variable in a simple procedure. One way to introduce this idea may be to use a procedure written by the teacher, as described in 'How we grow' in Chapter 7.

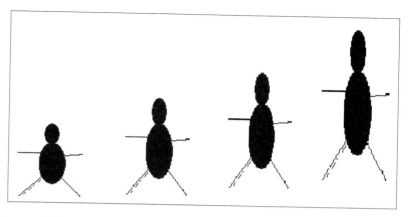

FIGURE 50

---

**Key mathematical ideas in this activity (Key Stage 1)**

- understanding the language of comparatives *Using and Applying Mathematics 3a*
- relating numerals and mathematical symbols to a range of situations *Using and Applying Mathematics 3b*
- recognising simple patterns and relationships, and making predictions about them *Using and Applying Mathematics 4a*
- using simple fractions in context *Number 2c*
- using a basic calculator and reading the display *Number 3e*
- describing and discussing shapes *Shape, Space and Measures 2a*

---

## *Key Stage 2*

As children's fluency with number increases, they will be able to use the idea of scaling with more precision. One way of extending the activities with 'Body measures' described in Chapter 7 is to use them as the basis for children to make simple scale models of themselves. Using a basic puppet design children can make models from cardboard and paper fasteners which are a half or a quarter of their own size (figure 51). They could use a calculator to work out each of the sizes they need for their models, or, if their measurements are recorded on a spreadsheet, they could use a formula to change all the measurements at once.

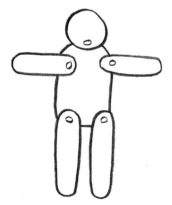

FIGURE 51

Once these miniature people have been created, they make a good support for creative writing about being shrunk in size, since they provide a tangible reference point for comparisons.

FIGURE 52  *A quarter-size model*

More sophisticated notions of scaling might involve working not just with children's own body measurements, but considering average measurements from a group of children.

'A visit to the theatre to see *The Nutcracker* was the starting point for a class of nine- and ten-year-olds to create a "rat world", in which everything was as big as it would seem if they were shrunk to the size of rats. They used a corner of the corridor near their classroom, and decided to fill it with the kind of rubbish rats might find attractive: a crisp packet, an empty drink can, a half-eaten sandwich.

Their teacher Amanda introduced the idea of a scale factor, to allow them to calculate the dimensions of the objects they wanted to make. Owen, Steven and Kim were given the task of finding what this scale factor should be. They realised that they needed to know the size of a human and the size of a rat, but they couldn't agree which of their heights they should use. Steven felt that it should be his, as he was the tallest. Owen thought that Kim's height would be better as she was "in the middle".

They took their problem to Amanda, who put it to the whole class to discuss. Several children supported Owen's idea that they needed someone whose height was somehow representative of the class as a whole, neither too tall nor too short. Amanda was able to develop this idea to remind them of some work they had done in science where they used the average of several measurements to get a more accurate figure. She suggested that the group could use the spreadsheet to help them find the average height of children in the class.

While Kim and Owen organised all the children to measure their heights, and enter the results on the computer, Steven went to the library to find out more about the size of rats. He found a reference book that gave the length of a rat as an average figure. When they had all the data they needed, their teacher helped them to use the spreadsheet to work out the scale factor (figure 53).

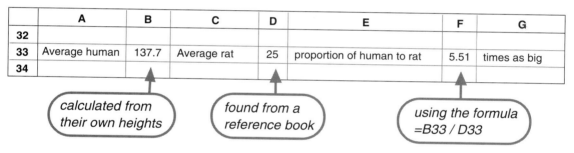

|    | A | B | C | D | E | F | G |
|----|---|---|---|---|---|---|---|
| **32** | | | | | | | |
| **33** | Average human | 137.7 | Average rat | 25 | proportion of human to rat | 5.51 | times as big |
| **34** | | | | | | | |

*calculated from their own heights*    *found from a reference book*    *using the formula =B33 / D33*

FIGURE 53

Other groups then used this information to plan the scale models they wanted to make. Claire and Davinder measured a crisp packet, and then used a calculator to increase the size by the scale factor. As they began to create the giant packet, they found that they needed to go back to the original and make more measurements to help them place the design on the packet correctly.'

---

**Key mathematical ideas in this activity  (Key Stage 2)**

- selecting and using appropriate mathematics *Using and Applying Mathematics 2a*
- using a measure of average *Handling Data 2c*

**(Key Stages 3 and 4)**

- developing an understanding of scale and enlarging shapes *Shape, Space and Measures  3d*

## Scaling in Logo

Drawing the same picture, but in different sizes, is a natural opportunity to introduce the idea of a variable in Logo. The need to scale up or scale down a drawing may arise through something which children are doing in their projects, or it might be introduced deliberately through a task set by the teacher. Stories such as The Three Bears provide a good context, although older children may feel this is beneath them. However, the idea of creating a family of characters might still be appealing.

There are two ways to change the size of drawings in Logo. Drawings in which all the lengths are the same (such as a square, a circle, a star) can be scaled by writing the procedure to include a variable for the length, as described in 'Making changes' in Chapter 4.

Within children's projects drawings are likely to be more complex, involving many different lengths, like Dylan's picture of a mouse (figure 54).

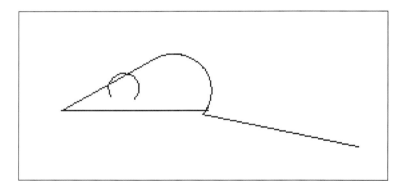

FIGURE 54

In order to produce a family of mice, Dylan would need to use a scaling factor, which is used to adjust all the lengths in the picture in the same proportion. Dylan's procedure began like this:

```
to mouse
lt 90
fd 110
rt 150
fd 80
repeat 81[fd 1 rt 2]
...
```

To make mice of different sizes, he would need to multiply all the lengths by the same amount.

```
to bigmouse :size
lt 90
fd 110 * :size
rt 150
fd 80 * :size
repeat 81[fd 1* :size rt 2]
...
```

Now **bigmouse 7** will produce a giant mouse. Baby mice could be made by multiplying by amounts less than one. So, **bigmouse .5** will produce a half-size mouse, and **bigmouse .2** an even smaller one.

Children's first reaction may be that they need to divide the lengths in order to make smaller mice, so they may want to write a procedure like this:

```
to babymouse :size
lt 90
fd 110 / :size
rt 150
fd 80 / :size
repeat 81[fd 1 / :size rt 2]
...
```

In fact **babymouse** and **bigmouse** are mathematically equivalent. **babymouse .5** would draw a large mouse: it would have the same effect as **bigmouse 2**. However, the idea of dividing by a fraction is probably more difficult to understand than multiplying by a fraction.

There are some difficult ideas here, but in Logo it is easy for children to experiment and get a feel for what is happening, so that the mathematical ideas are linked to a visual image. Some children may feel that they should also scale the angles, and experimenting with that can help them get a sense of the mathematical meaning of **similarity.**

---

### Key mathematical ideas in this activity  (Key Stage 2)

- selecting and using appropriate mathematics *Using and Applying Mathematics 2a*
- developing the use of the four operations to solve problems *Number 4a*

> **(Key Stages 3 and 4)**
>
> - appreciating the use of letters to represent a variable
>   *Algebra 2a*
> - developing an understanding of scale and enlarging shapes
>   and mathematical similarity *Shape, Space and Measures  3d*

# DOUBLING AND HALVING

## *Key Stage 1*

Doubling and halving numbers seems to 'make sense' naturally to children, long before they begin to think formally about multiplication and division. Doubles are often the first number bonds which children learn, and they form a good basis for building other number facts. For example, 'I know that five and five makes ten, so five and six must be one more, that's 11.'

A calculator or a spreadsheet can offer ways of extending and formalising children's knowledge of doubles and halves, and perhaps making links between addition and multiplication.

Working with a calculator, it makes sense to think about different ways of getting the same answer. We know that three and three make six, but how do we get the calculator to work it out? Children will probably most naturally use

$3 + 3 =$

Once they have this algorithm securely, they can use it to explore what happens when they double larger numbers. For example, what if you double thirty-three? Or 103? Once children begin to recognise some patterns, it's exciting to be able to predict results and confirm them with the calculator.

Another way of talking about doubles is to say 'two threes' instead of 'three and three'. Telling the calculator to work out two threes might be a way of introducing the multiplication symbol, and the calculator will also allow children to check for themselves that this new method really works:

| | | |
|---|---|---|
| $3 \times 2 =$ | gives the same result as | $3 + 3 =$ |
| $5 \times 2 =$ | gives the same result as | $5 + 5 =$ |
| $33 \times 2 =$ | gives the same result as | $33 + 33 =$ |
| $100 \times 2 =$ | gives the same result as | $100 + 100 =$ |

and so on. (Notice that I have chosen to translate 'two threes' as 'three times two' ($3 \times 2$). Other people might translate it as 'two times three' ($2 \times 3$). It is a matter of choice which you prefer.)

Working on a spreadsheet gives another valuable experience of expressing formally the process of doubling. Again a pattern of doubles could be made in different ways.

'Graeme had spent some time showing his class of seven-year-olds how they could tell a spreadsheet to work out a calculation. They used a time when the class were gathered around the computer to let different children type in two numbers, and then put a formula in another cell, while the rest tried to predict the outcome.

When he felt that the children were confident with how to set up a formula, Graeme gave one group the challenge of making a pattern of doubles on the spreadsheet. They chose to make two identical columns of numbers, and then use the third column to add them together, putting the formula = A1 + B1 in cell C1. They began typing similar formulas into the rest of column C, but Graeme intervened to show them how to fill the formula down the column. They were delighted with this trick, even though it took a few goes to get the hang of it.

| | A | B | C |
|---|---|---|---|
| 1 | 1 | 1 | 2 |
| 2 | 2 | 2 | 4 |
| 3 | 3 | 3 | 6 |
| 4 | 4 | 4 | 8 |
| 5 | 5 | 5 | 10 |
| 6 | 6 | 6 | 12 |
| 7 | 7 | 7 | 14 |
| 8 | 8 | 8 | 16 |
| 9 | 9 | 9 | 18 |
| 10 | | | |

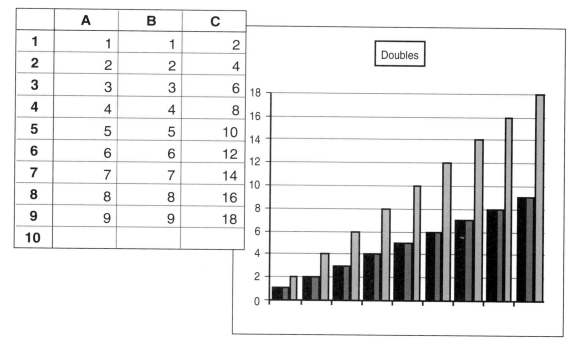

FIGURE 55

When they showed the pattern they had made to the rest of the class, Graeme encouraged them to make a graph (figure 55). They highlighted all three columns, and made a bar graph. It took them some time to really understand the graph they got: each group of three bars showed one row of the spreadsheet, with two bars the same height, and then one twice as long. Several of the class used the idea of steps or a staircase to describe what they saw.'

Looking at the graph alongside the tables of figures gave these children a different view of the pattern they had made. To develop the activity, groups might work on a range of different projects:

- extending the range of numbers going up to twenty or beyond in columns A and B;
- making a pattern of triples, and looking at the graph that makes;
- trying to make the doubles pattern in different ways.

Halving as a formal operation is less accessible than doubling for most children. A display of numbers and their doubles, whether it is generated on a spreadsheet or recorded by hand from calculator investigations, can form a starting point for drawing attention to the way the pattern can be read backwards to look at halves.

Although halving is the inverse of doubling, it is not natural to link halving with subtraction: you have to know what the half is, in order to know what to subtract to get it! A few children may be ready to be introduced to the division key on the calculator, and that 'divide by two' is a way to find a half. They may be able to link this to experiences with odd and even numbers, though of course they will inevitably come up against decimal notation if they explore dividing by two with a calculator.

---

**Key mathematical ideas in this activity  (Key Stage 1)**

- selecting and using the appropriate mathematics  *Using and Applying Mathematics 2a*
- developing different approaches  *Using and Applying Mathematics 2 c*
- recognising simple patterns and relationships *Using and Applying Mathematics 4a*
- exploring and recording patterns in addition and in multiples, using them to make predictions *Number 3b*
- using a basic calculator and reading the display *Number 3e*

---

## Key Stage 2

Older children may be able to extend the activity of doubling to begin to look at very large numbers. Starting points for this kind of activity can be taken from a number of myths and stories.

'Zelda and Anita (aged 10) wrote this version of a story Anna told them.

> ## The Story About Archimedes
>
> One day a King had a problem, so he sent for a man called Archimedes. People kept giving him Gold that was really lead. The King said to Archimedes, "if you solve my problem I will give you anything you would like!"
>
> Archimedes solved the problem and what he asked for was for the King to put 1 grain of rice on one square of a chessboard and 2 on the next then 4 on the next each time doubling and doubling for ever and ever to the end of the chessboard. The King at this point was saying "well I am glad that he has not asked for alot." [OR HAS HE !]

The children were intrigued by the problem of why Archimedes had made this request, and Anna helped them to set up a spreadsheet to find out what would happen (figure 56). They used three columns for the number of the square on the chessboard, the grains of rice on that square, and the running total of the number of grains. They needed to use a formula in each column to generate all the numbers they wanted.

|   | A | B | C |
|---|---|---|---|
| 1 | Square | Grains | Total |
| 2 | 1 | 1 | 1 |
| 3 | =A2+1 | =B2*2 | =C2+B3 |
| 4 | =A3+1 | =B3*2 | =C3+B4 |
| 5 | =A4+1 | =B4*2 | =C4+B5 |
| 6 | =A5+1 | =B5*2 | =C5+B6 |
| 7 |  |  |  |

|   | A | B | C |
|---|---|---|---|
| 1 | Square | Grains | Total |
| 2 | 1 | 1 | 1 |
| 3 | 2 | 2 | 3 |
| 4 | 3 | 4 | 7 |
| 5 | 4 | 8 | 15 |
| 6 | 5 | 16 | 31 |
| 7 | 6 | 32 | 63 |
| 8 | 7 | 64 | 127 |
| 9 | 8 | 128 | 255 |
| 10 | 9 | 256 | 511 |
| 11 | 10 | 512 | 1023 |
| 12 | 11 | 1024 | 2047 |
| 13 |  |  |  |

FIGURE 56

As they filled down the columns, the children were excited to see the numbers getting longer and longer, but soon they realised that something odd was happening. Further down the columns, some of the numbers looked strange. Anna explained that this was a way that mathematicians write very large numbers, known as scientific notation. At this point it didn't seem appropriate to go into detail about this, but the children discovered that they could make the columns of the spreadsheet wider, so that most of the numbers appeared as they expected, even though they had as many as nineteen digits.

*[A technical note: these children were using* ClarisWorks. *Other spreadsheets may deal with very large numbers differently.]*

Zelda noticed that there were some patterns in the numbers in the second and third columns: "The number in the middle column is one more than the one before in the end column." When she shared this with the class, other children had spotted different patterns. Nick thought that the numbers in column C were almost the doubles of column B, but one less. He needed to check some of the larger numbers with his calculator to make sure, but he was excited to find that some of the numbers on the spreadsheet were too big to fit in his calculator!'

The numbers which appeared on the spreadsheet in this activity quickly got so large that the children did not know how to read them, and it was very hard to get any sense of what they meant. The number of digits in the number gave some sense of their relative sizes, but the spreadsheet also offered the possibility of using graphs to get a picture of the numbers.

'In a class discussion, Anita made a graph of the numbers of grains on each square of the spreadsheet (figure 57). The children (and Anna) were very surprised by what they saw. At first many of them thought that the computer had "gone wrong", but gradually they began to make sense of it.

"The numbers up the side are those funny numbers."

"The real numbers would take too much room to write down."

"The first numbers don't show up because they are too small."

"They really shoot up at the end."

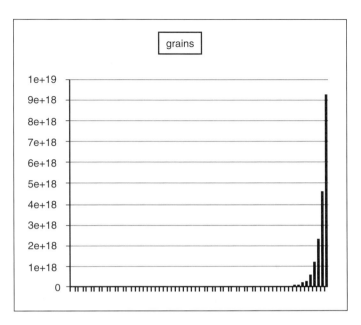

FIGURE 57

Because none of the early numbers showed on this graph, Anna suggested that they should try graphing just the first few numbers in the table. Eventually they graphed the first twenty rows of the "grains" column and the "total" column (figure 58). The results were another surprise, and prompted a lot more discussion and speculation.'

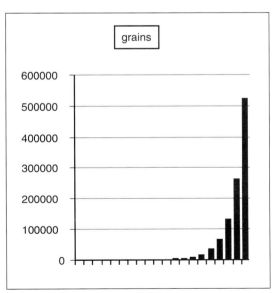

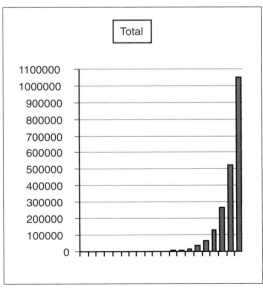

FIGURE 58

Anna found that she was carried along by the children's enthusiasm, and got rather out of her depth with the results they found. At the time she felt rather alarmed that she couldn't explain everything that was happening, but afterwards she realised that the children learnt a lot from trying to make sense of the graphs themselves, and listening to their attempts gave her some valuable insights into their thinking.

The same kind of activity could be used to look at numbers getting smaller and smaller as they are halved. Children might enjoy inventing their own stories to fit the mathematical situation. The investigation could be carried out with a calculator, using ÷ as a **constant function** (see Chapter 1). Looking at how the numbers change will extend children's experience with place value notation in decimals, although they would probably find the activity of graphing the results by hand too difficult.

---

**Key mathematical ideas in this activity  (Key Stage 2)**

- selecting and using the appropriate mathematics  *Using and Applying Mathematics 2a*
- using graphs and simple algebraic symbols  *Using and Applying Mathematics 3b*
- searching for patterns  *Using and Applying Mathematics 4b*
- making general statements, based on evidence they have produced *Using and Applying Mathematics  4c*
- extending their understanding of the number system *Number 2b*
- understanding and using the features of a basic calculator *Number 3h*

---

# LARGE AND SMALL NUMBERS

## *Key Stages 1 and 2*

Creating 'function machines' which make numbers grow or shrink is an activity which can be adjusted to the needs of children at any age. Similarly there are many ways in which a function machine can be created.

Younger children will probably enjoy making a physical machine from a cardboard box, which a machine operator can sit inside (or behind) to carry out the given function on numbers passed to her on slips of paper.

Equipping the operator with a calculator may speed up the operation of the machine, and increase the range of input numbers the operator can handle. The value of using the constant function soon becomes apparent.

Older children may be happy to work with a machine drawn on paper, where it may be easier to record the inputs and outputs in a systematic way (figure 59).

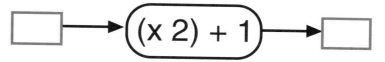

FIGURE 59

Children who have access to Logo or to a spreadsheet could use either of these application to create function machines on the computer (see descriptions in Chapters 3 and 4). Different skills and ideas are used in the two contexts: if you could arrange it, it would actually be very valuable for children to experience both approaches and think about the differences.

Working on the computer offers the advantage that the input and output numbers can easily be recorded and used to generate other ways of looking at the results. On a spreadsheet, the results could be graphed: in Logo, they might be used to produce a turtle drawing. An example is given in the next section.

Activities arising from the idea of a function machine can be focused in a number of ways. Making the function a secret so that others have to guess the rule is a familiar idea. Another focus might be to explore which functions or rules make numbers grow, and which make them shrink. Can children find any general patterns?

## LOOPED MACHINES

These are particularly good for looking at whether numbers grow or shrink when a particular function is used. The idea is simply that the output number is put back in as the next input (figure 60).

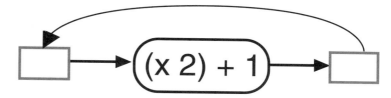

FIGURE 60

Creating looped machines on the computer is fairly simple, and very effective in generating lots of examples. The spreadsheet Zelda and Anita made in 'Doubling and halving' is actually a looped function machine. The examples in figure 61 give the structures for looped machines carrying out the function (×**2**) + **1** on a spreadsheet and in Logo.

<table>
<tr><td></td><td>**A**</td><td>**B**</td></tr>
<tr><td>1</td><td>**Input**</td><td>**Output**</td></tr>
<tr><td>2</td><td></td><td>=(A2*2)+1</td></tr>
<tr><td>3</td><td></td><td>=(A3*2)+1</td></tr>
<tr><td>4</td><td></td><td>=(A4*2)+1</td></tr>
</table>

```
to pop :number

if :number > 100 [stop]

pr :number

pop (:number *2) +1

end
```

FIGURE 61

In the procedure **pop** the second line will stop the procedure when the value of number gets bigger than 100. Obviously you can adjust this to suit the function, and the number of examples you want to generate. (See 'Again and again' in Chapter 4 for more detail of procedures like this which use tail recursion.)

As it stands, pop will just print out a list of numbers. Children might enjoy using these to make a turtle design, which will also give them a different image of the effects of the function machine. The design in figure 62 was made by adding **fd :number rt 90** to the third line of the procedure pop, and typing **pop 2.**

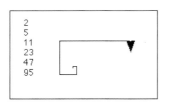

FIGURE 62

As children explore the effects of different functions, they will hopefully begin to form some general ideas, such as 'functions that involve addition make numbers grow'. Questions to pose next might be:

- Does it matter what number you start with?
- Does it matter what you add on (or multiply by, or take away)?

Children who begin to explore making numbers shrink will come up against two different kinds of results. Repeated subtraction will take them into negative numbers: repeated division will take them into more and more places of decimals.

In the course of these investigations, children may discover some functions which behave rather differently. For example, a looped machine using the function ÷ **2 + 1** starting at 10 produces the following list of values:

```
10
6
4
3
2.5
2.25
2.125
2.0625
2.03125
2.015625
2.0078125
2.00390625
2.001953125
2.0009765625
2.00048828125
2.000244140625
```

What happens if you choose a different starting number?

The numbers do continue to get smaller, but they have a finite limit. However long we go on for, the result will not go lower than 2. More able children may be interested to explore functions which behave in this way, although it is not a mathematical topic they would normally meet until much later in secondary school.

---

### Key mathematical ideas in this activity  (Key Stage1)

- asking 'what would happen if ...'   *Using and Applying Mathematics 4b*
- understanding general statements *Using and Applying Mathematics 4c*
- exploring and recording patterns in addition, subtraction and multiples *Number 3b*
- using a calculator and reading the display *Number 3e*
- understanding the four operations on number *Number 4a,b*

### (Key Stage 2)

- searching for patterns *Using and Applying Mathematics 4b*
- making general statements, based on evidence they have produced *Using and Applying Mathematics 4c*
- extending their understanding of the number system to include negative numbers and decimals *Number 2b*
- understanding and using the features of a basic calculator *Number 3h*

# CHANGING SHAPES

| length | width | area |
|---|---|---|
| 12 | 8 | 96 |
| 10 | 10 | 100 |
| 15 | 5 | 75 |
| 14 | 6 | 84 |
| 19 | 1 | 19 |
| 11 | 9 | 99 |
| 19.5 | 0.5 | 9.75 |
| 17 | 3 | 51 |
| 16 | 4 | 64 |
| 8 | 12 | 96 |
| 3 | 17 | 51 |
| 1.5 | 18.5 | 27.75 |
| 12 | 8 | 96 |
| 1 | 19 | 19 |
| 8.5 | 11.5 | 97.75 |
| 20 | | 0 |
| 20 | | 0 |
| 20 | | 0 |
| 20 | | 0 |
| 20 | | 0 |
| 20 | | 0 |
| 20 | | 0 |
| 20 | | 0 |
| 20 | | 0 |
| 20 | | 0 |
| 20 | | 0 |
| 20 | | 0 |
| 20 | | 0 |

FIGURE 63

## Key Stage 2

Working with shapes which grow or shrink can be an interesting source of number patterns, and some examples are given in Chapter 9. A different kind of activity arising from changing shapes is to look at maximising (or minimising) one aspect of the shape. For example, if you have a loop of string which measures 40 cm, how can you use it to enclose the largest area?

An example which may be more accessible for children is to limit the range of possible shapes to rectangles. Children might then tackle the investigation in a number of ways.

* Using squared paper, they could cut out possible examples, and count squares to find the area. The cut-out shapes could then be arranged in order of area.
* A development of this approach might be to calculate the areas, using a calculator if appropriate, which might mean that the rectangles no longer need to be drawn accurately.
* An alternative method of recording results would be to keep a table, showing the length, width and area for each rectangle (figure 63). If this table is kept on a spreadsheet, a formula can be used to calculate the area and there are more possibilities for exploring the data in different ways.

From looking at the table, children may begin to notice some patterns:

* the length and the width always add up to 20, which is half the total perimeter;
* when the length gets one bigger, the width gets one smaller;
* the biggest widths seem to give the biggest areas.

Sorting the data into order might make it easier to see these patterns, and looking at graphs may also add to the overall picture. The graph in figure 64 seems to illustrate the third statement.

'Jordan and Stellios had made this graph, and wondered what would happen if they went on making the width of the rectangles bigger. Jordan started to draw another example with width 11, but Stellios stopped him. "If the width is 11, the length will be 9. I can work it out. You take it away from 20." They added this data to their spreadsheet, and then realised that they could work out any examples they wanted.

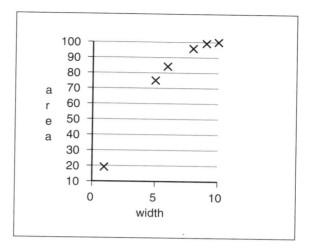

FIGURE 64

Their teacher, Penny, decided that she wanted to push them to go a little further. She suggested that they tried to teach the spreadsheet their method for calculating the length, once they had chosen the width. It took them some time to get a formula that worked. Penny needed to help them to turn "take it away from 20" into an instruction that the spreadsheet could understand. Eventually they got the formula =20 – B8 in cell A8, and were happy that this gave the correct result.

Penny reminded them about filling the formula down the column, and they typed in many more widths, trying fractions as well as whole numbers. When they eventually looked back at the graph, they were quite surprised by what they saw (figure 65).

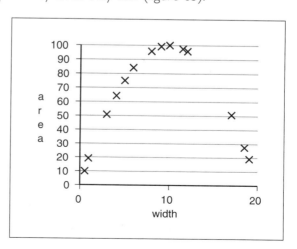

FIGURE 65

After some discussion, they realised that the maximum value for the area was in the middle of the graph, which was actually a square. Other groups around the room had reached the same answer through different approaches. Penny was pleased with the way the children had been able to work on this activity at different levels, and began collecting other similar questions and problems they could work on.

* What if the loop of string was 30 cm long? or 50 cm?
* A farmer has 30 m of fencing, and wants to make a rectangular pen for some sheep against a wall. How can she make the biggest pen?
* What is the largest open box you can make from a sheet of A4 paper, using this method? (Figure 66)

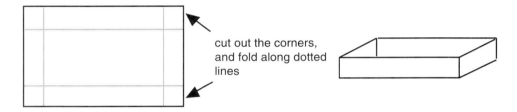

cut out the corners, and fold along dotted lines

FIGURE 66

This last question linked well to a topic on waste and recycling the class were going to do next term. Penny realised there would be lots of other opportunities to look at different kinds of packaging.'

---

**Key mathematical ideas in this activity  (Key Stage 2)**

* using graphs and algebraic symbols *Using and Applying Mathematics 3b*
* searching for patterns in results *Using and Applying Mathematics 4b*
* finding perimeters, areas and volumes *Shape, Space and Measures 4c*
* understanding and using the features of a basic calculator *Number 3h*
* collecting and representing data, interpreting a wider range of graphs *Handling Data 2b*

**(Key Stage 3)**

* constructing formulae relating to real-life situations *Algebra 3b*

# *9*

# EXPLORING PATTERNS

There is nothing exceptional about the range of activities described in this chapter. They have been deliberately chosen to be familiar, but what *is* different is the way in which the addition of IT can transform the mathematical experiences of the children.

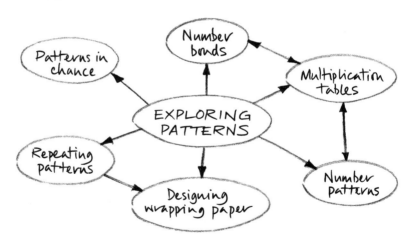

# NUMBER BONDS

## *Key Stage 1*

Exploring the patterns in number bonds, for example all the ways of making 10, is an activity which young children may approach in many ways. Different kinds of practical activities, counting games and rhymes will all contribute to children's fluency with number bonds. Finding lots of possible ways of making 10 encourages children to think flexibly and make links between addition and subtraction. Using a calculator can allow children to check results and explore using a wider range of numbers. For example, 10 is 15 minus 5, and also 115 minus 105.

Looking at number bonds graphically can add a further dimension to children's images of number. The graph in figure 67 shows a pattern of the pairs of numbers which add to make 10.

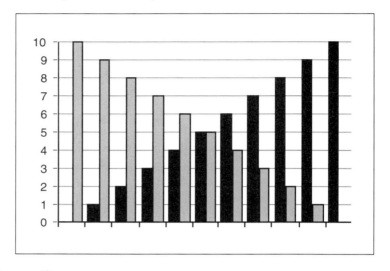

FIGURE 67

Discussing the symmetry in the graph, and the patterns in the table of numbers from which it was drawn, could help to consolidate children's ideas about commutativity.

This graph was drawn from data recorded on a spreadsheet. The children entered pairs of numbers which they thought added to 10 in two columns. Their teacher had helped them put a formula into the third column to add the pair of numbers, and so check the total. Of course the graph could have been drawn by hand, which would have taken much longer and required other skills.

As children's fluency with numbers increases, they might go on to use the spreadsheet in other ways, exploring different ways of using formulae to generate the patterns. For example, pairs of numbers which add to 13 could be generated by starting with 13 and using a formula to subtract consecutive numbers, starting at 1.

**Key mathematical ideas in this activity  (Key Stage 1)**

- recognising simple patterns and relationships *Using and Applying Mathematics 4a*
- asking questions, such as 'what would happen if ...' *Using and Applying Mathematics 4b*
- exploring and recording patterns in addition and subtraction *Number 3b*
- learning addition and subtraction facts *Number 3c*

# MULTIPLICATION TABLES

## *Key Stage 2*

Multiplication tables are a rich source of number patterns; the patterns in the units digits, digital sums, and relationships between different tables are just some of the possibilities. Generating multiplication tables on a calculator or computer can extend these activities, and open up new possibilities for looking at patterns.

How could you generate multiples of three:

- with a calculator, using the constant function?
- with a Logo procedure?
- on a spreadsheet?

If you have never tried these activities, it would be worth exploring them yourself before using them in the classroom. They each require different approaches and offer different insights into the underlying mathematics. None of these approaches will find the patterns for you, but they will all generate examples quickly (once you have found an algorithm that works) and provide you with plenty of data to work on.

In 'doubling and halving' in Chapter 8, there is a description of how some seven-year-olds worked with the two times table on a spreadsheet. The following case study extends this idea.

'"Can you make a spreadsheet so that you have the one times table in one column, the two times table in the next, then the three times table, and so on?" This was the problem Hilary set for some nine-year-olds in her class. They had some experience with using formulae, and she wanted to let them try out their own ideas before discussing the activity with them.

Zoe and Sally set off confidently. They typed the first column of numbers, but decided this was going to take too long, so they used a formula in column B (figure 68).

| | A | B | C | D |
|---|---|---|---|---|
| **1** | 1 times | 2 times | 3 times | 4 times |
| **2** | 1 | 2 | | |
| **3** | 2 | =B2*2 | | |
| **4** | 3 | | | |
| **5** | 4 | | | |

FIGURE 68

They got the result they expected in B3, but were very surprised when they filled the formula down the column.

Helen and Jessica used a different approach. Like Zoe and Sally, they typed in the one times table, but then they multiplied the first column by two to get the two times table. They had the formula =A3 * 2 in B3.

Jon and Michael had yet another method. They made the first column by starting with one, and then used a formula to add one in each row. They extended this to make the next column by adding two each time, the next by adding three, and so on. Michael was excited to find that the finished product was like the ready reckoners they used for multiplication: he had never seen the connection before!

Hilary encouraged the children to share their ideas, and although it took Zoe and Sally some time to understand what their method was actually doing, they ended up with formulae that worked, and decided to extend their columns beyond ten times.

Hilary showed them how to make a line graph of the columns they had produced (figure 69).

As they discussed it, she raised a number of questions.
- Where would the line for six times be?
- What tables would give a line between the two times and three times lines?
- How could you make a steeper line, or a flatter line?
- What is the steepest line you could make?

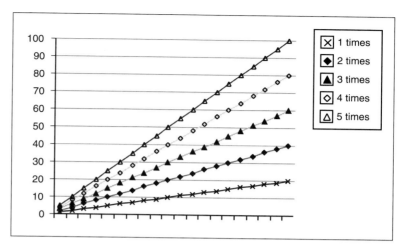

FIGURE 69

She also challenged the children to explore with some of these new ideas (such as making the four-and-a-half times table) and look at the patterns they could see in the results.'

Hilary's final question proves to be rather confusing when you try to explore it on the computer. The children's response was to put in a really big table, like 100 times, but when they graphed this, they were disappointed (figure 70).

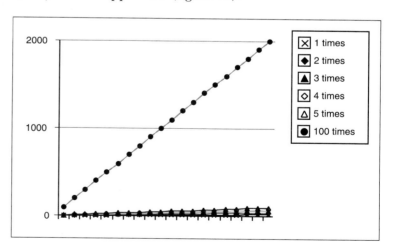

FIGURE 70

The 100 times line does not seem to be any steeper than the five times was on the first graph. This is because the computer has automatically adjusted the scale: notice how the original lines are all bunched together at the bottom of the graph. To get a real sense of how steep the 100 times line is, you would need to fix the scale of the graph to be the same as the original. You would then also have to stretch the new graph vertically in order to see all the lines properly.

---

**Key mathematical ideas in this activity (Key Stage 2)**

- understanding and using the language of relationships like 'multiple of', 'factor of' *Using and Applying Mathematics 3a*
- using graphs and algebraic symbols *Using and Applying Mathematics 3b*
- searching for patterns in their results *Using and Applying Mathematics 4b*
- making general statements based on evidence they have produced *Using and Applying Mathematics 4c*
- exploring number sequences, explaining patterns and simple relationships *Number 3a*
- consolidating knowledge of number facts *Number 3c*
- understanding relationships between addition and multiplication *Number 3f*

---

# NUMBER PATTERNS

## *Key Stage 2*

There are many good sources for work on number patterns, often arising from practical situations, patterns with shapes and so on. It would not be appropriate to give lots of examples of this kind here, but it is worth mentioning some ways in which the use of calculators and computers might help to extend children's thinking, as well as providing powerful tools for generating examples.

The constant function on a calculator is one such tool, which allows children to look at the effect of repeating an operation. Here are some further challenges.

- Use a 'post-it' strip to cover up all of the display except the units digits. Try to make the **units** give these patterns
  0, 5, 0, 5, ...   6, 3, 6, 3, ...   2, 7, 2, 7, ...
  Can you make them all? Try to explain why you can or can't make the patterns. What other patterns can you make?
- Now cover everything except the tens. Can you make the **tens** give these patterns?
  1, 1, 2, 2, ...   1, 3, 5, 7, ...
- Use two calculators. One person starts from 0, and adds 5. The other starts from 50 and takes away 4. Will they ever arrive at the same number?
  Try different patterns. Can you make sure the patterns always meet? or never meet?

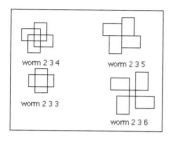

FIGURE 71

In Chapter 8, there are examples of how Logo and spreadsheets can be used to make function machines, and to explore looped machines. There is also an example of how the resulting number pattern could be drawn with the turtle. Here is another activity, using number trios, for which Logo makes a useful tool.

The activity is often known as 'Worms'. Take three numbers: make a design by moving the length of the first number, turning through a right angle, moving the length of the second number, and so on. Repeat until you get back to your starting point (figure 71).

As you can see from these examples, very different designs arise from different number trios.

- What other trios would give a design with a hollow centre like worm 2 3 6?
- How do you make overlapping designs like worm 2 3 4?
- Are there any trios that don't produce closed designs?
- Can you predict the kind of design any trio will make?

This investigation is a rich one. It could take a long time to get to a point of being able to answer the final question. The advantage of using Logo as a tool is that many examples can be explored quickly. The procedure to draw the worms is a simple one, using three variables. However, in these examples the **forward** command multiplies each variable by ten to make the designs a reasonable size.

---

**Key mathematical ideas in this activity  (Key Stage 2)**

- understanding and using the language of relationships *Using and Applying Mathematics 3a*
- searching for patterns in their results *Using and Applying Mathematics 4b*
- making general statements based on evidence they have produced *Using and Applying Mathematics 4c*
- exploring number sequences, explaining patterns and simple relationships *Number 3a*
- consolidating knowledge of number facts *Number 3c*
- understanding relationships between operations *Number 3f*
- understanding and using the features of a basic calculator *Number 3h*

# REPEATING PATTERNS

## *Key Stage 1*

Graphics software can provide an alternative medium for creating repeating patterns with shapes and colours, offering the additional possibility of building up the design by **copying** (or **cutting**) and **pasting**. This is an important technique which is used in many different applications; word processing, spreadsheets, databases as well as graphics. The technique involves **selecting** objects on the screen, for example, words, drawings or cells in a spreadsheet, which you then want to move or reproduce somewhere else.

Once the objects are selected, you can choose to make a **copy**, or to **cut** them from that place on the page. You can then go to another place on the page, and **paste** the objects in their new position. This technique operates slightly differently in different applications, and particularly in painting and drawing software. You will need to experiment yourself before introducing the idea in the classroom.

Using copying and pasting to make repeating patterns has two advantages. It enables children to produce a pleasing finished result in a short space of time. More importantly, it focuses attention on what unit of the pattern is repeated. The pattern in figure 72 could be made by copying each shape separately, or more efficiently by copying the largest unit of the pattern.

FIGURE 72

In addition, the children will be practising the use of an IT skill which will be valuable in many contexts in the future.

---

**Key mathematical ideas in this activity (Key Stage 1)**

- recognising simple patterns and relationships *Using and Applying Mathematics 4a*
- using repeating patterns to develop ideas of regularity and sequencing *Number 3a*

# DESIGNING WRAPPING PAPER

## *Key Stage 2*

Exploring repeating patterns can be extended with older children to involve ideas of geometrical transformations. The following case study is based around wrapping paper, but wallpaper and decorative friezes could also provide the stimulus for similar activities.

'After Christmas, Andy presented his class with a box of pieces of wrapping paper as a resource for sorting activities. He allowed each group some time to explore the designs using whatever criteria they chose for sorting, which were generally based on colour or the content of the motifs – holly, bells, Christmas trees, and so on.

With the whole class he discussed the idea of a motif, and the way in which most of the designs were built up by repeating one or two motifs. He concentrated on a couple of examples. In one, the motif was spaced out in staggered lines, giving a diagonal design. In the other, the motif was repeated with alternate versions turned upside down. He then asked the groups to sort the paper samples again, this time concentrating on how the patterns were built up, rather than other factors.

Some children found it quite hard to ignore the superficial similarities between some of the designs, but others began to see the different ways in which the motifs were placed on the paper. As he talked to the groups, Andy introduced some geometrical terms to describe the patterns. Eventually, the class identified three different ways in which a motif could be copied: a translation, which meant simply moving it along; a reflection, which meant flipping it over; and a rotation, which meant turning it upside down.

Andy used graphics software to demonstrate these three transformations. Many of the wrapping paper designs (Christmas trees, bells, stars, candles) were symmetrical, so Andy chose an irregular shape which allowed the children to see the transformations clearly (figure 73).

Over the next couple of weeks, the children experimented with designing their own wrapping paper for a particular occasion. Andy gave them the choice of working on the computer, or in other media, such as paint or crayon, using templates.

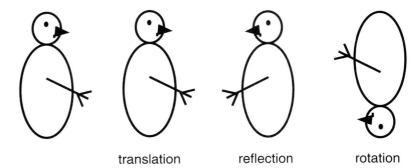

translation          reflection          rotation

FIGURE 73

Matthew and Tim worked with graphic software to make a design using balloons and the words "Happy Birthday". They were excited to find that they could use instructions to reflect or rotate the words as well as the pictures. Once they had made one line of their design, they realised that they could use copying and pasting to extend their design quickly.

Shanta and Vicki chose to work in Logo. They wrote a procedure to draw a parcel. They found that they could rotate their motifs quite easily by turning the turtle before they began drawing, but they needed another procedure to move the turtle to the right place for each drawing, and they sometimes lost track of which way the turtle was facing. Andy introduced them to the commands SETPOS and SETH to control the position and heading of the turtle.'

When the children had spent some time working on their wrapping paper designs, Andy asked them to evaluate the different media they had used. In the discussion, they came up with a number of different points.

- Some children liked working with paint and crayons, because they could use colours, which weren't available on the computer. Others printed out their computer designs, and coloured them in by hand.
- Working with graphics software, the children found they could rotate and reflect their motifs easily, and use copying and pasting to continue their design quickly.
- Some children were dissatisfied because they could not space their motifs out accurately in the graphics software, and the finished designs looked wobbly. The same was true for some of the designs made by hand. Other children didn't really think this was a problem.

- The children who worked with Logo used a procedure to overcome the problem of spacing, so their designs sometimes looked neater, but they felt it was more difficult to draw the original motifs. Many children felt that drawing by hand was the best way to create the motifs.
- Although it was easy to rotate motifs in Logo, producing reflections was more difficult. None of the children really solved the problem; they simply used rotations in their design instead.

This last point raises some interesting mathematical issues, and Andy planned to return to it later, to extend the children's ideas of symmetry. One way to approach the activity would be to get the children to play turtle, working in pairs where one turtle tries to move as a mirror image of the other. From this experience, the children will hopefully realise that the second turtle needs to turn in the opposite direction from the first. So, in order to make a reflection in Logo, you would need to write a new procedure with left and right turns reversed.

---

**Key mathematical ideas in this activity  (Key Stage 2)**

- trying different mathematical approaches _Using and Applying Mathematics 2b_
- developing strategies and overcoming difficulties _Using and Applying Mathematics 2c_
- transforming 2-D shapes by translation, reflection and rotation, and visualising movements and transformations to create and describe patterns _Shape, Space and Measures 3a_
- using co-ordinates to specify location _Shape, Space and Measures 3b_

---

# PATTERNS IN CHANCE

## Key Stage 2

When exploring probability, children need to have the experience of collecting data from random events such as tossing coins or throwing dice. In order to look properly at the patterns in the results you really need a fairly large quantity of data, but the novelty of repeating experiments can soon wear off.

'Yvette wanted to give her class of ten- and eleven-year-olds experience with looking at the patterns in large collections of data. She organised the children to work in pairs, on two activities. Each pair had to toss a coin and throw a die, and record the results of 60 experiments. They worked on the activities in odd moments between other work.

When one or two pairs had finished, Yvette showed the class a spreadsheet she had set up so that they could enter their results from both experiments. The running totals were kept at the bottom. At several points during the week, Yvette asked children to make graphs of the totals so far, and print these out. They made bar graphs of the dice experiment, and pie charts for the coins (figure 74).

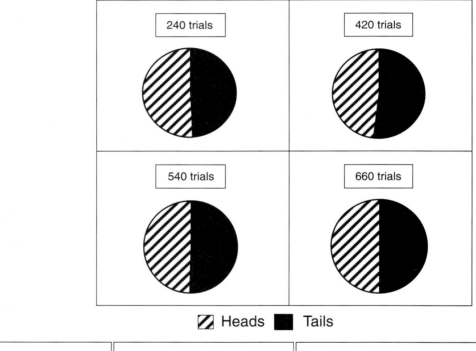

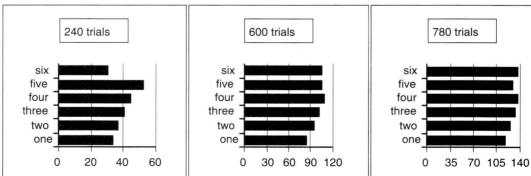

FIGURE 74

When they looked at the collection of graphs, the children discussed how the results seemed to change, and finally settle down to a recognisable pattern.'

One of the most difficult aspects of understanding probability for most people is reconciling the two ideas that random events are unconnected with those which have gone before (the coin doesn't *remember* that it landed heads last time), and the idea that over a large number of trials, regular patterns emerge. Discussing a series of graphs like these can help children to get a sense of the cumulative effects of taking larger and larger numbers of trials.

---

**Key mathematical ideas in this activity  (Key Stage 2)**

- presenting information and results clearly *Using and Applying Mathematics 3c*
- collecting and representing data appropriately *Handling Data 2b*
- drawing conclusions from statistics and graphs and recognising why some may be uncertain or misleading *Handling Data 2d*
- developing an understanding of probability, discussing events and experiments *Handling Data 3a*
- recognising situations where probabilities can be based on equally likely outcomes *Handling Data 3c*

---

## Make your own lottery

Many children are fascinated by the National Lottery, and other similar gambling games. Understanding the structure of how these games operate on may have a positive influence on views of the pros and cons of gambling, which may counteract some teachers' worries about the ethical issues involved.

Many computer applications, for example Logo and some spreadsheets, include the facility to generate random numbers, which could be used in projects to create simulated gambling games. The details of how the random function works will vary, but generally the user puts in a number to fix the range from which the random number is chosen. In some cases **random 5** will give a number between 1 and 5, in other cases it may give one between 0 and 4.

A simple model of the National Lottery would be to choose a random number between 1 and 49 six times, but of course this will allow the possibility of picking the same number more than once. Creating a Logo procedure or a spreadsheet to overcome this problem may be beyond the capabilities of primary children, but it might make a good challenge for adults!

# CHAPTER 10 VEHICLES

The purpose of this chapter is
- to show you some examples of how activities within the topic of *Vehicles* can be developed to enrich children's mathematical thinking.

There is nothing exceptional about the range of activities described in this chapter. They have been deliberately chosen to be familiar, but what *is* different is the way in which the addition of IT can transform the mathematical experiences of the children.

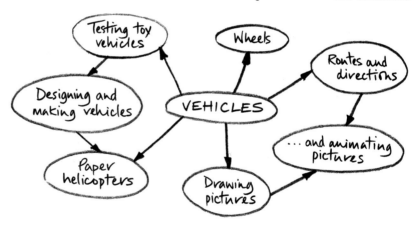

## ROUTES AND DIRECTIONS

### Key Stage 1

How do you find your way around the classroom, the school, the neighbourhood? Could you explain to a visitor how to get to the playground, or help a new child find the toilets?

Questions like these provide a stimulating starting point for activities of planning routes, giving directions and eventually making maps and plans. There is a lot of scope for children to practise directing each other, and gain confidence in how to make their instructions clear. But the problem with using humans is that they use their common sense. They know that they need to stop when they meet a wall, whatever you have told them to do, and they will turn in the appropriate direction when they can see a sign on the toilet door, without worrying about having been told to go the other way.

Giving directions to a robot like *Roamer, Pip* or *Pixie*, or to a turtle on the computer screen, is a bit like talking to a person, but it gives a real purpose to making your directions precise. All of these robots respond to the same basic set of commands in order to move forward or backward, or to turn left or right. Each instruction has to be accompanied by a number to say how far the robot is to move, or how far it should turn. Some information about the differences between the robots is given in the introduction to Chapter 4.

Children need some time to explore these commands and to get a sense of how the robot moves and turns. Don't worry if the children don't already know about degrees: they will quickly get used to using these special numbers, and get a sense of how they affect the robot. It probably won't take too long for someone to find out that 90 is a particularly useful number.

---

**Key mathematical ideas in this activity  (Key Stage 1)**

- relating numerals to practical situations  *Using and Applying Mathematics 3b*
- asking 'What would happen if?' *Using and Applying Mathematics 4b*
- getting a sense of the relative sizes of numbers *Number 2b*
- beginning to see angle as a measure of turn *Shape, Space and Measures 3b*
- estimating and comparing distances using non-standard units *Shape, Space and Measures 4a*

---

## *Extending the activity with robots*

A new challenge will encourage children to develop their confidence with controlling the robot. For example, they could try to park the toy under a chair, or negotiate a simple obstacle course. Stories that involve journeys, such as *We're going on a Bear Hunt* (Rosen and Oxenbury, 1989), or *Bears in the Night* (Berenstain, 1973), lend themselves to more elaborate scenarios for the robot to move around. The scenery doesn't need to be elaborate; it can be sketched out by children on the back of sheets of wallpaper, or chalked on an area of playground.

As well as entering instructions singly, you can give the robot a list of commands to carry out a more complex journey. This provides a further challenge as children need to plan several movements in advance. It is a good idea to record the sequence of commands in some way, by writing it down or by using pre-prepared cards, so that children can revise their instructions if they do not work first time.

---

**Key mathematical ideas in this activity  (Key Stage 1)**

- recognising relationships and making predictions  *Using and Applying Mathematics 4a*
- asking 'why?'  *Using and Applying Mathematics 4b*
- using forms of mathematical presentation *Number 3d*

---

## Extending the activity with the screen turtle

Controlling the movements of a screen turtle presents new challenges. The numbers that are needed to control turtle movements are generally larger, and the direction of turns is more difficult to judge when you cannot physically stand next to the turtle. Ideally, children might benefit from using a robot before they move onto the screen turtle, but don't be put off if you haven't got access to one. Most children get on well with the turtle, though they may need to spend time 'playing turtle' themselves to help establish left and right turns.

If the size of the numbers required is a serious problem, it is possible to write some simple procedures to make the turtle move in larger steps – see examples given in Chapter 4. The screen turtle also moves very quickly, and if this proves to be a problem try the suggestions given in Chapter 4 to slow its movements down.

Moving the turtle around a prepared scene on the screen makes a good introductory activity, and it can be less frustrating for beginners than drawing a picture. You can set the turtle to have its pen up so that it does not draw for these activities. A scene for the turtle can be created in a number of ways.

- You (or some older children who are experienced with Logo) could draw a scene, or perhaps a maze, or a race track, in Logo. This could be saved as a procedure so that it could be re-created for children to drive their turtle around.

'Rosemarie created the scene in figure 75 for her class of six- and seven-year-olds, using *LogoWriter*. It is based on *We're going on a Bear Hunt*. Children worked in small groups taking the turtle around the screen and through the various obstacles; splashing through the river, stumbling through the wood and so on.'

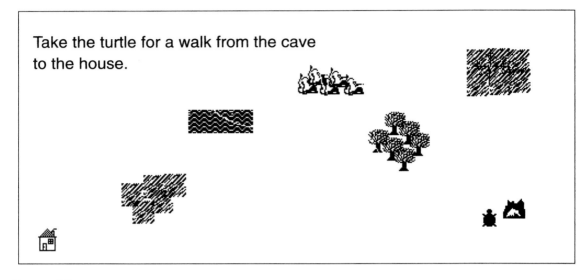

Take the turtle for a walk from the cave to the house.

FIGURE 75

- Depending on the version of Logo and the computer you are using, it may be possible to *import* a picture which has been created in a graphics package, and use this as a background for the turtle's journeys. This might make it possible for children who are beginners with Logo, but familiar with other applications, to make their own scenes for the turtle. The maze in figure 76 was made by some six-year-olds, using *ClarisWorks* graphics.

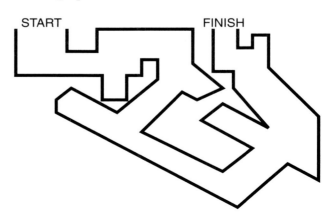

START          FINISH

FIGURE 76

- A different approach is to draw out a scene on an acetate sheet (the kind used on overhead projectors) and fix it on to the computer screen.

Whichever approach you choose, moving around a prepared scene offers a purposeful activity for learning to control the turtle. As children become more confident with their instructions, they can be encouraged to type in a list of commands for a complete journey. Again, it is a good idea to encourage children to make a record of their instructions so that they can be modified later. (This may be a situation in which it is appropriate to slow the turtle's movement down, or to show the children how to get the turtle to wait at certain points, to allow for story telling. See Chapter 4.)

---

**Key mathematical ideas in this activity (Key Stage 1)**

- recognising relationships and making predictions *Using and Applying Mathematics 4a*
- asking 'why?' *Using and Applying Mathematics 4b*
- using forms of mathematical presentation *Number 3d*
- working with larger numbers *Number 2b*

---

## Key Stage 2

Further challenges involving giving directions to a screen turtle might be appropriate for children who have more experience with Logo. Creating a set of directions for a whole journey provides a good context for introducing the idea of writing procedures, which can be stored and modified. This allows for much more complicated movements to be included, such as the turtle following a curved path. The following ideas might stimulate projects which involve giving more sophisticated routes and directions.

- Creating a maze, and then programming the turtle to move through it.
- Using two, or even more turtles to move together; perhaps they might be having a race, or performing a dance, or chasing each other.
- Creating a scene with several elements – perhaps a shop, a school, a park – and writing procedures to send the turtle from its 'home' to each of them. So, if I type **park** there will be a procedure that takes the turtle to the park.

All of these projects, and particularly the last one, will bring children up against the problem of returning the turtle to a fixed starting point before the procedure is run. Normal turtle commands are not efficient for doing this, as they always relate to the turtle's current position. In Logo it is also possible to use co-ordinates to give the turtle's position, and this might be an appropriate way to introduce this idea to children. Using co-ordinates in Logo is described in Chapter 4. Because the origin (i.e. the point (0 0)) of the co-ordinate grid is at the centre of the screen, you have to use negative numbers to place the turtle in some areas. This can provide a very useful context for children to explore the ideas of co-ordinates and of negative values, because the computer provides immediate feedback about the effects of the numbers they have chosen.

Some of the activities described here overlap with activities involving animating pictures, which are discussed later in this chapter.

---

**Key mathematical ideas in this activity (Key Stage 2)**

- planning and extending a task  *Using and Applying Mathematics 1b*
- trying different approaches; deciding what you need to know *Using and Applying Mathematics 2b*
- developing strategies and ways of overcoming difficulties *Using and Applying Mathematics 2c*
- working with negative numbers *Number 2b*
- using co-ordinates to specify location *Shape, Space and Measures 3b*
- using degrees to measure turn *Shape, Space and Measures 3c*

---

# DRAWING VEHICLES

## *Key Stage 1*

Making drawings of vehicles is likely to form part of the work on this topic for children of any age. Such drawings might be done for a number of purposes, and address a range of skills. Making drawings using the computer will engage children in some mathematical thinking which may not occur when they create pictures in other media.

## ADDING WHEELS

Drawing vehicles with wheels can lead easily to children thinking about some properties of circles. Using a graphics package, a curve is generally given as a drawing tool, but making the curve into a circle can provide an opportunity to talk about what makes circles special (figure 77).

FIGURE 77

Adding spokes to the wheel may require some thought about diameters, the centre of the circle, right angles and dividing angles equally. When drawing by hand, there is often no need to think explicitly about any of these, but using a graphics package, where lines can easily be moved, deleted or re-drawn, again offers an opportunity to talk about the mathematical aspects of the drawing.

For some drawings, the whole wheel may not be visible, so only a part of the circle is needed. In some drawing packages, children will discover a tool for drawing curved lines, which can be used to make quarter circles. Some children seem to be able to use this very effectively, even though most adults seem to find it rather confusing!

Of course, some children will avoid the problem of wheels altogether in their drawings (figure 78).

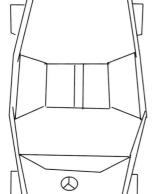

FIGURE 78

## DRAWING VEHICLES WITH LOGO

Producing a drawing of a vehicle in Logo can be quite a lengthy task, particularly if children get absorbed in the sort of detail which many of them delight in. As work may need to extend over more than one session, this can be an appropriate time to introduce the idea of writing **procedures** as a way of saving work. Generally children need to be encouraged to find an efficient way of moving from drawing on the screen to writing procedures in the **editor**.

A sensible approach to begin with is to keep a record on paper of the commands that are used, and then add these to the procedure as each part of the drawing is completed satisfactorily. This allows the possibility of experimenting and making mistakes, without having to start from scratch each time something goes wrong. The aeroplane in figure 79 was drawn by some seven-year-old children, using this approach. They needed to experiment in direct drive to choose the correct angles before they wrote the final procedure.

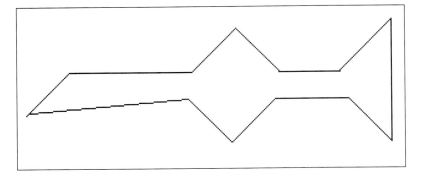

FIGURE 79

When children become more experienced with using the editor, they may be encouraged to write separate procedures (sometimes known as **sub-procedures**) for different parts of the picture, and to combine these in one overall procedure. This means that, for example, a procedure to draw a wheel could be used more than once in the overall picture, or the procedure for drawing a boat used several times in a picture of a yacht race.

Adding wheels in a Logo drawing will bring children up against the problem of how to make the turtle move in a circle. They may have already come across the need to move in other than straight lines in their work with *Roamer, Pip* or *Pixie*. Whether they are working on the screen or with a robot, it will probably be helpful for them to 'play turtle', and think how they might walk around a circle. The need to go 'forward a bit' and then 'turn a bit' many times provides a good opportunity to introduce **repeat** as a short-cut. The instruction **repeat 360 [fd 1 rt 1]** will produce a circle, but of course there are many other combinations of numbers which will also work. Children will need to experiment to find a circle of a suitable size.

> **Key mathematical ideas in this activity  (Key Stage 1)**
>
> - developing different mathematical approaches, and overcoming difficulties  *Using and Applying Mathematics 2c*
> - discussing their work responding to mathematical questions *Using and Applying Mathematics 3c*
> - describing and discussing shapes that can be seen or visualised *Shape, Space and Measures 2a*
> - recognising and using geometrical features of shapes *Shape, Space and Measures 2c*
> - estimating using units of length and angle *Shape, Space and Measures 4a*

# ANIMATING PICTURES

## *Key Stage 2*

Although pictures can be created in many media, a unique feature offered by the computer is the ability to create animations. In some versions of Logo, such as *LogoWriter*, the shape of the turtle can be changed, so that it can look like a car, a lorry, a train, a rocket, or anything else you can design. This opens up the possibility of writing scenarios in which vehicles move against a background picture.

'Leah and Parandeep created an animation around an airport scene. It is difficult to convey on paper what an animated project is like, but figure 80 shows several stages in the scene. The first action is the bird flying across the top of the sky. Next the helicopter takes off, flies at low level above the waiting crowd, flies up in front of the buildings, turns and flies back, finally landing on its pad.

In creating their animation, the children had to solve several problems. They needed to position the bird and the helicopter to begin their action. Then, to create the sense of animation, they had to make the turtles move at different speeds. They started by using **repeat 40 [fd 5 wait 5]** to move the helicopter across the screen, but it took quite a lot of experimentation to get the appearance of smooth movement, and to adjust the speed of the flight at different stages of the journey.

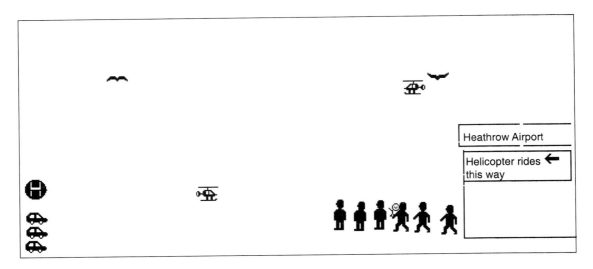

FIGURE 80

Another problem they tackled was to make the bird appear to flap its wings. They did this by creating two shapes for the turtle, one with its wings down, and the other with them up, and alternating these for each short movement of the turtle (see Chapter 4).

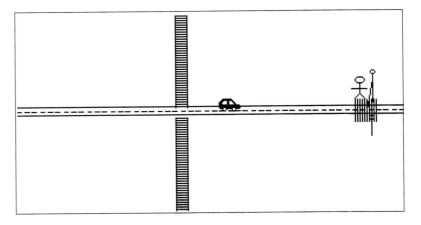

FIGURE 81

Ric and Sanjay made this "story-picture" using two turtles. The car moves along the road until it reaches the zebra crossing. Then it stops to allow the pedestrian to walk across before continuing its journey. Finally, a train moves along the track. Using two turtles posed additional problems, as they had to consider the sequence of the movements.'

> **Key mathematical ideas in this activity  (Key Stage 2)**
>
> - planning and extending a task  *Using and Applying Mathematics 1b*
> - trying different approaches; deciding what you need to know *Using and Applying Mathematics 2b*
> - developing strategies and ways of overcoming difficulties *Using and Applying Mathematics 2c*
> - using multiplication and division in breaking down distances  *Number 3e*
> - using co-ordinates to specify location *Shape, Space and Measures 3b*

# TESTING TOY VEHICLES

## *Key Stage 1*

Exploring the performance of different toy vehicles, or perhaps of the same vehicle in different conditions, is an activity that links closely to children's experiences. It also provides a natural context for introducing scientific and mathematical ideas. A simple test to set up in the classroom is to run vehicles down a slope, and measure how far they travel.

FIGURE 82  *How far will it go?*

You could record the results of the tests on paper, but putting them onto a spreadsheet or a database will allow children to draw graphs of the results quickly and easily. This has two real benefits. In the short term, looking at a graph can give some children a much clearer picture of what has happened than looking at a list of figures. They may begin to get an understanding of why graphs can be useful and not just decorative. In the longer term, it is giving children practice at reading a graph in a situation where the information it contains is familiar to them. This helps them to see the connections between the experiment, the data and the graph, and can be a very powerful factor in helping to develop the ability to interpret graphs.

'The children set up a slope to test the collection of toy vehicles that they had brought in from home. As each group took a turn, they used different methods to measure the distances that the vehicles travelled. Some did it by counting the tiles on the floor. Others made rods of multilink cubes, and measured with these, or paced out the distances in foot lengths. Each group recorded their results on a spreadsheet. This meant that they could easily produce a bar chart, which gave a different way of looking at their results (figure 83). Jodi's group used floor tiles to measure how far each vehicle travelled.

|  | A | B | C | D |
|---|---|---|---|---|
| 1 |  | Jodi | Chris | Anna |
| 2 | Blue car | 5 | 4 | 4 |
| 3 | Red car | 3 | 1 | 5 |
| 4 | Bus | 6 | 6 | 5 |
| 5 | small bus | 1 | 1 | 1 |
| 6 |  |  |  |  |
| 7 |  |  |  |  |
| 8 |  |  |  |  |
| 9 |  |  |  |  |
| 10 |  |  |  |  |
| 11 |  |  |  |  |
| 12 |  |  |  |  |
| 13 |  |  |  |  |
| 14 |  |  |  |  |
| 15 |  |  |  |  |

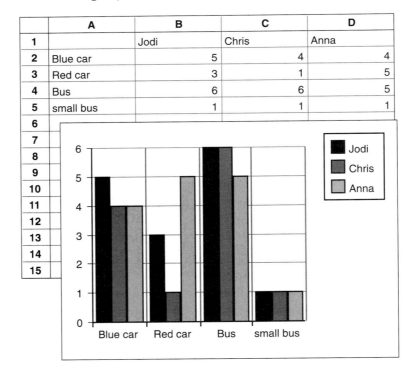

FIGURE 83

When the class came together to share what they had been doing, the teacher was able to focus their attention on a number of issues. Often each child in the group had taken a turn, so there were several results for each vehicle. These usually were not the same, and so they had to discuss how to make their tests fair. Another idea which some children found more difficult was that sometimes a test was spoilt, and had to be disregarded. For example, in the results from Jodi's group shown in figure 83, when Chris tested the red car it bumped into the leg of a chair. The children's attention was on taking turns, and they felt it wasn't right for Chris to get an extra go at testing, so they included his result even though they knew it was inaccurate.'

The results of such tests could be recorded on a database, and graphs drawn in a similar way. However, it needs a little more thought to decide the best way to organise the data. Each test carried out would need to be a separate record. For the example shown above, the record would have to contain three fields: the vehicle, the distance travelled, and the name of the tester.

| | |
|---|---|
| **vehicle** | blue car |
| **distance** | 5 |
| **tester** | Jodi |
| **vehicle** | blue car |
| **distance** | 4 |
| **tester** | Chris |
| **vehicle** | blue car |
| **distance** | 4 |
| **tester** | Anna |
| **vehicle** | red car |
| **distance** | 3 |
| **tester** | Jodi |

From these records, a bar chart could be drawn of the vehicles and the distances they travelled.

Many other kinds of tests might be carried out: running vehicles on a variety of surfaces, putting different loads in a toy lorry, comparing wind-up toys, or other kinds of propulsion, and so on.

> **Key mathematical ideas in this activity  (Key Stage 1)**
>
> - discussing work and asking mathematical questions
>   *Using and Applying Mathematics 3c*
> - using different forms of representation   *Using and Applying Mathematics 3d*
> - collecting, recording and interpreting data, using tables and graphs *Number 5b*
> - using non-standard or standard units to measure length
>   *Shape, Space and Measures 4a*

## Key Stage 2

The idea of testing vehicles can be extended with older children to focus on the specific factors which affect how a vehicle travels. A simple slope provides a fair way of propelling the vehicle, so that other factors can be varied.

'A class of nine- and ten-year-old children were posed the question, "What affects the way a toy car travels down a slope?" They began by playing with some cars in order to develop their ideas. They came up with a long list of factors which they thought might be important.

- the length of the car
- the weight of the car
- the size of the wheels
- the distance between the wheels
- the height of the slope
- whether the car had an axle or not
- how smoothly the wheels turned
- what the wheels were made of
- the surface of the slope or the floor

In order to make the experiments manageable, their teacher organised each group of children to explore just one of these factors, using their understanding of fair testing to keep all other factors the same. This was easier to do for some factors than others!'

For this kind of investigation, the key idea is to change one variable (size, weight, height, etc.) and see how this affects the performance of the vehicle, which can be measured by the distance or the time it travels. Recording results on a spreadsheet or database gives the opportunity for drawing graphs which may give further insight into the results and into how the experiment may be developed. The most appropriate graph for comparing two variables is a scattergraph.

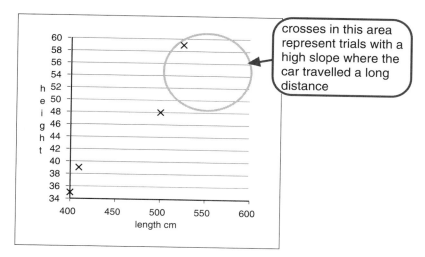

FIGURE 84

The graph in figure 84 shows results from testing the same car on slopes of different heights. Each cross is the result of a single experiment, and the actual data about the height of the slope and distance the car travelled can be read off on the axes. The main value of the graph is that the overall pattern of the crosses shows the relationship between the two variables: in this case it looks as though the distance the car travels increases as the slope is made higher.

'Andy, Sharon and Julie produced the graph in figure 84 after they had made four trials in their experiment. The overall pattern confirmed their initial feeling that the car would go further when the slope was higher, but they decided that they needed to make some more trials with the slope at heights between 40 and 50 cm and between 50 and 60 cm, to check that the pattern really held.

Later, their graph showed a rather different pattern (figure 85). The overall trend was still clear, with the distances increasing fairly steadily as the height of the slope was increased, but there were two "rogue" points near to the top of the graph. It seemed that when the slope became very high, the car did not travel so far. After some discussion, Sharon was able to give an explanation for this; she said, "When the slope is really steep, the car bounces at the bottom, so it doesn't go very far."

Another group chose to look at how the weight of the car might affect its performance. They used one car, but changed its weight by adding lumps of Plasticine. They needed to weigh the car accurately between experiments, and their teacher took the opportunity to discuss how to get the weight to the nearest gram. In measuring how far the car travelled, they needed to use the same skills of accurate measurement with different units. On one occasion they wanted to record a distance of ninety-six-and-a-half cm. The spreadsheet will not accept fractions, so they had to convert this to 96.5 cm.

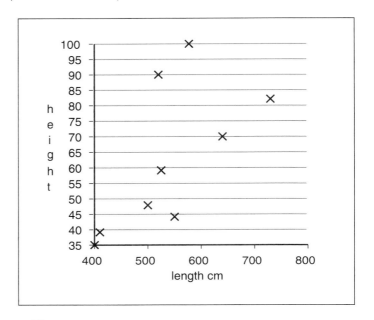

FIGURE 85

At the end of the activity they used the computer to write the report in figure 86, incorporating the graph they had produced and a picture to illustrate the activity.'

In making their graph, Richard's group had arranged their data so that the variable they were changing (known as the control variable) is on the horizontal axis, and the variable which changes because of this (the dependent variable) is on the vertical axis. This is the conventional way of presenting the graph, although graphs that are drawn the other way around – like Sharon's graph shown earlier – are not 'wrong'.

The children whose work is described here used spreadsheets for recording their results, but they could have used a database instead. Each trial would have to be a separate record, containing two fields: the weight of the car and the distance travelled. If you have a choice, a spreadsheet is probably easier to use, because the data can be entered more directly, and it is possible to see all the data on the screen at once.

## WEIGHT EXPERIMENT

RICHARD SAM TOM ROB CRAIG AND ANTHONY did an experiment on the weight of a car. We put loads of plasticene on the car to make it heavier To see if It made it go further or not. We put all the data on the car on the spreadsheet and saved it on a disk. We found out that The car went further when we added more weight.

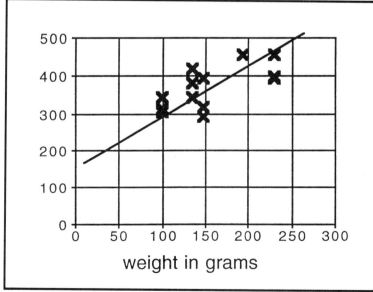

The line shows the trend on the scattergraph. On the scattergraph it shows you that the heavier the car the further it goes.

FIGURE 86

---

**Key mathematical ideas in this activity (Key Stage 2)**

- presenting information and results clearly *Using and Applying Mathematics 3c*
- making general statements based on evidence they have produced *Using and Applying Mathematics 4c*
- choosing and using appropriate measuring instruments and reading scales with increasing accuracy *Shape, Space and Measures 4b*
- collecting and presenting data appropriately, interpreting graphs *Handling Data 2b*
- drawing conclusions from graphs, and recognising why these can be misleading *Handling Data 2d*

---

# DESIGNING AND MAKING VEHICLES

## Key Stage 1

The skills which children may learn through testing toy vehicles can be extended to support projects in science and technology involving designing and making vehicles. When building a vehicle, particularly one made from Lego or some other construction set which can be easily dismantled and modified, children may want to try out and improve their designs.

'Rob made a paper plane and found that it flew better when he added a paper-clip to the nose. He decided to try adding more paper-clips, to see if this made it even better. His teacher encouraged him to record his results on a spreadsheet. Rob set up two columns to record the number of paper-clips (he did this by calling them plan(e) 1, 2, etc.), and how far the plane flew, measured in floor tiles. While he was working on this his teacher asked what he expected to happen. Rob said that he thought the more paper-clips he put on, the further the plane would fly.

When he drew his graph (figure 87), he was excited that the first few columns seemed to 'go up in steps', which he felt confirmed his expectation. However, he was puzzled by what happened after that. He shared his work with the class, and there was some discussion about why the graph looked as it did. A few children suggested that perhaps he had not launched the plane in the same way each time.

| | A | B |
|---|---|---|
| **1** | name | how far it travels |
| **2** | plane | 11 |
| **3** | plan 1 | 14 |
| **4** | plan 2 | 17 |
| **5** | plan 3 | 19 |
| **6** | plan 4 | 21 |
| **7** | plan 5 | 29 |
| **8** | plan 6 | 20 |
| **9** | plan 7 | 33 |
| **10** | plan 8 | 32 |
| **11** | plan 9 | 25 |
| **12** | plan 10 | 23 |

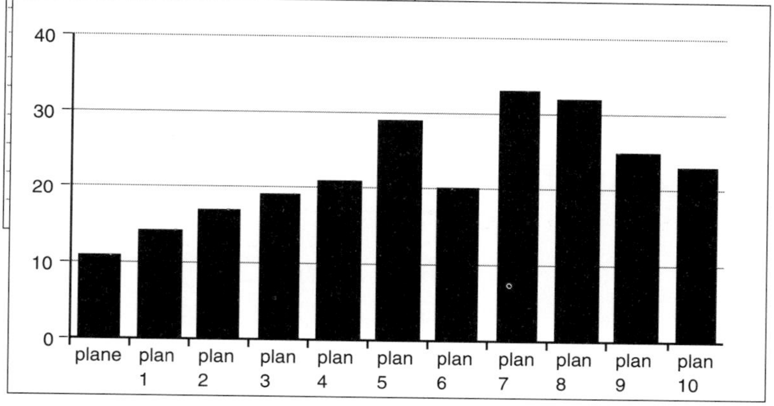

FIGURE 87

Although Rob had been able to understand and discuss the graph, he found scientific ideas about fair testing and experimental error difficult to grasp. His teacher was anxious to provide other experiences which would challenge him in this area.'

Paper planes present particular problems for fair testing because it is so hard to keep the launch constant. It may be easier to keep other variables constant with vehicles of other kinds. The list below gives some other examples of vehicles which children might test in the same way in order to find the best design. In each case the *control variable* can be treated as discrete, so that results can be shown on a bar chart similar to Rob's.

- Wind-up vehicles, made from cotton reels and powered by rubber bands can be tested to see the effects of the number of turns the band is given.
- Cars built from Lego can be made longer or taller or heavier, and tested down a slope.
- Different sized cardboard wheels can be fixed to the wheels of Lego cars.

> ### Key mathematical ideas in this activity  (Key Stage 1)
>
> - discussing work and asking mathematical questions  *Using and Applying Mathematics 3c*
> - using different forms of representation  *Using and Applying Mathematics 3d*
> - recognising simple relationships and making related predictions about them  *Using and Applying Mathematics 4a*
> - collecting, recording and interpreting data, using tables and graphs *Number 5b*
> - using non-standard or standard units of measurement *Shape, Space and Measures 4a*

# PAPER HELICOPTERS

## Key Stage 2

The process of designing, making and testing vehicles can be developed further with older children, and can provide opportunities for considering more sophisticated mathematical ideas. The following case study is based around making small paper 'helicopters' which spin when they are dropped and float down to the ground relatively slowly (figure 88).

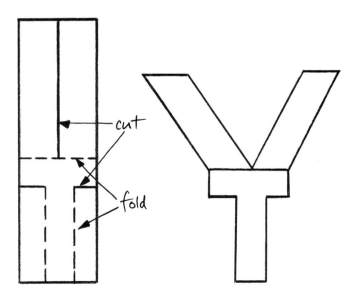

FIGURE 88

'The class were given the challenge of designing and making helicopters which would fly for as long as possible. They began by all making a helicopter, and experimenting with letting them fly. They soon realised that they needed to get as high up as possible to launch them. After this, Jean their teacher asked them to suggest ways in which they might change the design. They didn't have any trouble coming up with ideas:

- the length of the wings
- the length of the tail
- the kind of paper used
- adding paper-clips to the tail
- the width of the wings
- the shape of the wings

Jean organised the class into groups of three or four, and asked each group to plan an experiment to investigate changing one of these features. Some of the groups had clear ideas straight away. Hannah's group decided to make a helicopter with long wings, and then test it lots of times, cutting a bit off both wings between flights. Carol's group set off making helicopters all the same lengths, but with wider and wider wings.

Others found it harder to think about fair testing. Neil's group collected four different kinds of paper, and made a helicopter from each. The trouble was, they had used a whole piece of paper for each, and the pieces weren't all the same size. They found it hard to understand that they weren't making a fair test.

After some more discussion about launching their helicopters in the same way each time, and working out how to use the stopwatches, the children were ready to begin. Each group recorded their results on a spreadsheet, and their teacher encouraged them to use graphs to help them see some patterns in their results.

Hannah's group carried out their plan of starting with long wings, and gradually cutting bits off. Their first graph (figure 89) seemed to support their hunch that helicopters with longer wings would fly best.

However, there were some gaps in their graph as they hadn't been very systematic in the way they cut lengths off. After showing their work to the class, they carried out some more experiments, trying some longer wings, as well as some of the lengths they had "missed". When they looked at the graph again (figure 90), they saw a different pattern: it seemed as though the best length for the wings was "somewhere in the middle".'

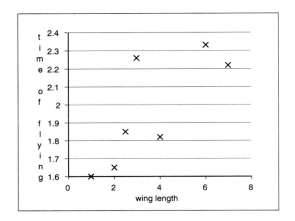

FIGURE 89

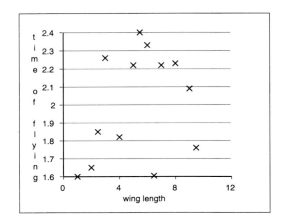

FIGURE 90

As with some of the other activities described in this chapter, the case study features the use of a spreadsheet, but the results could also have been saved on a database, with each experiment as a separate record.

The spreadsheet offered another facility which the children were able to use to improve their experiments.

'Some of the groups became a bit concerned about timing the flights of their helicopters. In fact, it was quite difficult for them to measure accurately because the periods of time were quite short. Sam's group were testing tail length. They experimented using two stopwatches, so that they got two different readings for each flight. These often differed considerably, depending on who was paying attention!

They were shown how to use the average function on the spreadsheet, and Jean suggested that they did each experiment three times, and then used the average of these results. She helped them set up an area on their spreadsheet to do this (figure 91).

| first test | second test | third test | average |
|---|---|---|---|
| 2.16 | 3.09 | 2.1 | 2.45 |

FIGURE 91

The children didn't know how to calculate the average, but they had a sense that it gave them a "better estimate" of the real time their helicopter flew. When they used the average values to draw their graph, they got a clearer picture of how the length of the tail affected how their helicopter flew. They came to the conclusion that middle-sized tails were the best.'

> **Key mathematical ideas in this activity (Key Stage 2)**
>
> - making general statements based on evidence they have produced  *Using and Applying Mathematics 4c*
> - choosing and using appropriate measuring instruments and reading scales with increasing accuracy *Shape, Space and Measures 4b*
> - collecting and presenting data appropriately, interpreting graphs *Handling Data 2b*
> - drawing conclusions from graphs, and recognising why these can be misleading  *Handling Data 2d*
> - using a measure of average  *Handling Data 2c*

# WHEELS

## *Key Stage 1*

Drawing vehicles is likely to be a common activity when children are working on this topic. Some mathematical possibilities arising from drawing wheels have already been discussed in the section 'Drawing vehicles' earlier in this chapter.

The work on 'Testing toy vehicles' also described earlier, could be extended to focus on wheels. If vehicles are made from Lego, or some other construction kit, it might be possible to test them with different numbers, or different sizes of wheels. Other vehicles that children have made might also be tested, but it could be harder to focus on the wheels, as there will be many other variables.

A related investigation could be to test the same vehicle on different surfaces, to see how its wheels respond.

'Claire and Edward chose to test a toy car which could be pulled back and then released. It took them some time to realise that they needed to make sure that they always pulled it back the same distance. They used rods made of 10 Unifix cubes to measure how far the car travelled on each test. They tested the car several times each on the floor in the corridor, recording their results on the computer, and using them to draw a bar graph.

After a class discussion about their test results, they realised that provided they pulled the car back the same distance each time, all the bars on their graph should be about the same length.

To extend the activity for them, their teacher suggested they tried the same test on the carpeted area of the classroom. Later they laid sheets of paper over the carpet to make a third test and were able to compare their results to decide which surface allowed the car to travel furthest.'

---

**Key mathematical ideas in this activity  (Key Stage 1)**

- discussing work and asking mathematical questions  *Using and Applying Mathematics 3c*
- using different forms of representation  *Using and Applying Mathematics 3d*
- collecting, recording and interpreting data, using tables and graphs *Number 5b*
- using non-standard or standard units to measure length *Shape, Space and Measures 4a*

---

## Key Stage 2

For children with more experience of measuring and handling numbers, wheels can provide a context for looking in more detail at properties of circles, and particularly at the relationships between radius, diameter and circumference. Recording results on the computer means that results can be graphed easily, but more importantly it allows children to cope easily with the awkward numbers which arise from their investigations.

'As part of a project on vehicles, Rebecca's group chose to look at the problem "If you know the size of a wheel, can you predict how far it will travel in one turn?"

They began by collecting some data from wheels they could find around the school (various toy cars, some bicycles, a spinning wheel, a wheel barrow). After some discussion, they decided to record the width of the wheel (i.e. its diameter), and the measurement around its rim (the circumference). The mathematical terms were new to them, but they were quite pleased to have some short labels for the columns in their spreadsheet.

The numbers they recorded didn't seem to show any pattern, so Lynda, their teacher, got them to make a scatter graph to look at how the two measurements varied. The crosses seemed to lie roughly on a straight line. When their class visited a transport museum, they managed to find more wheels to measure. Their final graph confirmed the earlier pattern (figure 92).

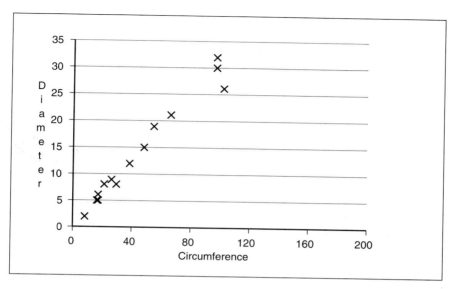

FIGURE 92

When they showed the graph to the class, they tried to describe their feeling that the two measurements were related. They felt that the straight line was significant, but it was still hard to see a pattern. They wanted to find a simple rule like "add 5 to the diameter" or "halve the circumference". Lynda intervened to suggest that they should try dividing the circumference by the diameter, to see how many times bigger it was. She helped them put a formula into the spreadsheet to do this for them (figure 93).

The column of results still was not very clear – some of their measurements hadn't been taken very carefully – but they could see that they were all around 3. After talking about problems with accurate measurement, the teacher was able to show them how the spreadsheet could work out the average of all the results, which gave a "better estimate".

These children were able to get some feeling both for the value of Pi – the rather magical number which relates the diameter and the circumference of a circle – and for one way in which a mathematical average might be useful, even though they did not yet know how to calculate it. The computer enabled them to work with data which they understood, even though the numbers involved were difficult.

| | A | B | C | D |
|---|---|---|---|---|
| 1 | Circumference | Diameter | Circ / Diameter | |
| 2 | 66 | 21 | 3.14 | |
| 3 | 16 | 5 | 3.20 | |
| 4 | 17 | 6 | 2.83 | |
| 5 | 97 | 30 | 3.23 | |
| 6 | 21 | 8 | 2.62 | |
| 7 | 38 | 12 | 3.17 | |
| 8 | 26 | 9 | 2.89 | |
| 9 | 97 | 32 | 3.03 | |
| 10 | 8 | 2 | 4.00 | |
| 11 | 102 | 26 | 3.92 | |
| 12 | 55 | 19 | 2.89 | |
| 13 | 29 | 8 | 3.62 | |
| 14 | 48 | 15 | 3.20 | |
| 15 | 17 | 5 | 3.40 | |
| 16 | | | | |
| 17 | | | Average | |
| 18 | | | 3.23 | |
| 19 | | | | |

FIGURE 93

**Key mathematical ideas in this activity (Key Stage 2)**

- making general statements based on evidence they have produced  *Using and Applying Mathematics 4c*
- choosing and using appropriate measuring instruments and reading scales with increasing accuracy *Shape, Space and Measures 4b*
- finding the circumference of circles and being introduced to the ratio $\pi$ *Shape, Space and Measures 4c*
- collecting and presenting data appropriately, interpreting graphs *Handling Data 2b*
- drawing conclusions from graphs, and recognising why these can be misleading  *Handling Data 2d*
- using a measure of average  *Handling Data 2c*

# FURTHER READING

## CHAPTER 1

Shuard, Hilary (*et al.*). *Calculators, children and mathematics,* Simon & Schuster, 1991

Lewis, Anna. *Starting from everday objects: starting points for work with calculators,* BEAM, 1993

## CHAPTER 2

*Fifty things to do with databases and spreadsheets.* Centre for Statistical Education. University of Sheffield, 1993

Green, David and Graham, Alan (eds). *Data handling, teaching within the National Curriculum,* Scholastic, 1994

Keeling, Roger and Whiteman, Senga. *Maths through Databases.* KW Publications, 1993

Lewis, Anna (*et al.*). *Starting from scratch: Data-handling (starting points for work on data-handling in the early years).* BEAM, 1993

Merttens, Ruth and Leather, Ros. *Handling data: photocopiable activities by the IMPACT Project (Key Stage 1).* Scholastic, 1994

Senior, Sue. *Data handling (Key Stages 1 and 2).* Owlet Books, 1990

## CHAPTER 3

Healy, Lulu and Sutherland, Rosamund. *Exploring mathematics with spreadsheets.* Simon and Schuster Education, 1992

Keeling, Roger and Whiteman, Senga. *Simply Spreadsheets.* KW Publications, 1990

*Fifty things to do with databases and spreadsheets.* Centre for Statistical Education, University of Sheffield, 1993

*Thinking about spreadsheets.* National Council for Educational Technology, 1990

# CHAPTER 4

Ainley, Janet and Goldstein, Ronnie. *Making Logo Work,* Blackwell, 1988

Blythe, Katrina. *Children learning with Logo, a practical guide to working in the classroom.* National Council for Education Technology, 1990

Hoyles, Celia and Noss, Richard (eds). *Learning mathematics and Logo.* MIT Press, 1992

Papert, Seymour. *Mindstorms: children, computers and powerful ideas.* Harvester Books, 1980

# CHAPTER 5

Jones, Lesley (ed.). *Teaching mathematics and art.* Stanley Thornes, 1991

Woodman, Anne and Albany, Eric. *Mathematics through art and design, 6-13.* Unwin Hyman, 1988